ELS

developed by Knowledge Schools Trust

Essential Letters and Sounds

ELS Fluency Teacher's Handbook

Written by Tara Dodson

Series Editors Tara Dodson and Katie Press

We aim for all children to read well, quickly.

OXFORD
UNIVERSITY PRESS

Great Clarendon Street, Oxford, OX2 6DP, United Kingdom

Oxford University Press is a department of the University of Oxford. It furthers the University's objective of excellence in research, scholarship, and education by publishing worldwide. Oxford is a registered trade mark of Oxford University Press in the UK and in certain other countries.

First published in 2025

British Library Cataloguing in Publication Data

Data available

978-1-382-07080-5

10 9 8 7 6 5 4 3 2 1

The manufacturing process conforms to the environmental regulations of the country of origin.

Printed in the UK by Bell and Bain Ltd, Glasgow

The manufacturer's authorised representative in the EU for product safety is Oxford University Press España S.A. of el Parque Empresarial San Fernando de Henares, Avenida de Castilla, 2 – 28830 Madrid (www.oup.es/en or product.safety@oup.com). OUP España S.A. also acts as importer into Spain of products made by the manufacturer.

Acknowledgements

Written by Tara Dodson
Illustrated by Kate McLelland
Series Editors Tara Dodson and Katie Press

The publisher would like to thank Herts for Learning for their contribution to the development of this programme.

The publisher and authors would like to thank the following for permission to use photographs and other copyright material:

Photos: p22, p28, p34, p40, p46, p52: Richard Cave Photography.

Artwork by Emily Cooksey, Natalie Vasilica, Gareth Conway, Tom Jellett, Claudia Ranucci, Richard Watson, Charlotte Cotterill, Beatriz Castro, Maxine Lee-Mackie, Cinta Villalobos, Ally Marie, Adriana Puglisi, Irina Avgustinovich, Craig Shuttlewood, Mackinzie Rekers, Berta Maluenda, Maxime Lebrun, Alex Patrick, Tania Rex, Amy Jindra, Adam Walker-Parker, Erin Brown, Andy Rowland, Cathrin Peterslund, Beth Hughes, Ciara Ni Dhuinn, Ella Hobbis, Lucy Semple, Eva Katinka Bognar, Sam Loman, Shabab Shamshirsaz, Alette Straathof, Robin Boyden, Yoss Sanchez, Veronica Montoya, Marina Perez Luque, Helen Morgan, Esther Hernando, Alex Paterson, Felicity Sheldon, Jack Viant, Daniel Hawkins, Aaron Cushley, Ashley King, Anna Aronson, Pauline Gregory, James Cottell, Tamara Anegon, Sarah Jennings, Lesley Danson, Samya Zitouni, Deborah Schreiber, Katie Kear, Ayesha L. Rubio, JiaJia Hamner, Blithe Fielden, Alexandra Colombo, Ruth Bennett, Elif Balta Parks, Hannah McCaffrey, Irina Mileo, Lia Visirin, Fatima Anaya, Davide Ortu, Kubra Teber, Makenzie McCarthy, Megan Higgins, Clau Souza, Uran Duo, Kofi Ofosu, Thaís Mesquita, Emma Allen, Aleksandar Zolotic, Aleksei Bitskoff, Shahab Shamshirsaz, Fanny Liem, Patrick Corrigan, Lilia Miceli, Howard Gray, Ceej Rowland, Steve May, Bea Tormo, Tatsiana Burgaud, Katie Abey, Ekaterina Tikhova, Daniel Duncan, Vincent Batignole, and Aga Maszota.

Every effort has been made to contact copyright holders of material reproduced in this book. Any omissions will be rectified in subsequent printings if notice is given to the publisher.

FSC www.fsc.org MIX Paper | Supporting responsible forestry FSC® C007785

Contents

Essential Letters and Sounds Fluency

Essential Letters and Sounds Fluency (ELS Fluency) supports the development of reading fluency and is designed to be used in conjunction with your ELS Phonics lessons in Year 1 and ELS Essential Spelling lessons in Year 2.

Fluency is a skill that comes with practice of code that children are already familiar with where there is repeated, specific and focused practice of the code that children can confidently apply.

When the code of the words in the texts is familiar to the children, their focus can turn from decoding to the comprehension of the text. Reading with fluency is the effortless decoding of words in conjunction with expressive reading which will, in turn, allow comprehension and interpretation of the text.

ELS Fluency is designed to support pupils to make this transition from decoding to comprehending. Once a 'fluent' reading of the text or grapheme is achieved, children's attention can then be focused on the meaning of the text. Whilst some pupils will comprehend the texts they are reading when they are overtly decoding and blending some text, this is not the case for all pupils.

ELS Fluency is built on the following principles to develop fluency for reading:

- repeated practice to ensure accuracy and improve the speed and ease of reading
- application of grapheme-phoneme correspondences (GPCs) that children are confident and familiar with to develop automaticity
- development of phrased, expressive reading (prosody) through reading aloud
- increased understanding of vocabulary and language to underpin comprehension
- modelled and repeated reading to support children's developing fluency.

How to use ELS Fluency

ELS Fluency sits outside of your phonics sessions, and is designed as a complement to phonics and spelling teaching.

These texts are not matched to the children's current phonic knowledge. Rather, ELS Fluency texts are designed to lag behind the current phonics teaching. As part of your normal practice, you will be assigning weekly texts matched to current knowledge – this supports their developing GPC knowledge. **Your ELS Fluency texts should lag six weeks behind this current knowledge.** Texts designed to support fluency are from earlier on in the progression and require children to know the code within the text so that they are not entirely focused on decoding and blending.

For example: If you are assigning a R1 Autumn 2 Week 4 decodable book to match the child's current phonic knowledge, they should be reading a R1 Autumn 1 Week 4 text for their fluency book.

Whilst children may be recognizing familiar words that they have decoded and read before, they may not be applying this deeper understanding when reading longer text extracts or books. Therefore, once children are confidently applying the taught code (usually many weeks after having been initially taught the GPCs) then they can use the Fluency Anthologies to support the development of their fluent reading. The Fluency Progress Checks (provided in this Handbook) can also be used to assess and plan next steps.

You can use both the anthologies of texts for ELS Fluency (*ELS Fluency Anthology 1*; *ELS Fluency Anthology 2*) to support children's fluency journey, along with the decodable texts that match ELS, as per the guidance within Essential Letters and Sounds.

> Children who are working on earlier GPCs will need to use a different fluency text from their peers. Therefore, Fluency can be used as a whole-class activity, but can also be used in smaller groups or 1:1 if more appropriate.
>
> ELS Fluency is designed to be flexible. This means that you can make use of it in the most appropriate way to support your learners.

Delivery

In general, we recommend that an ELS Fluency session takes place at least once a week as a whole-class activity. This will be where you model reading a text from the Fluency Anthologies with prosody.

Planning

Select the text from the Fluency Anthology which is at the correct level for your children (6 weeks behind current phonics knowledge – see the Fluency Progression on page 8 of this Handbook).

Ensure that you and every child can see the Anthology text.

Delivery step 1:

Allow the children a few minutes to read through the text independently.

You will read each sentence, line or phrase (determined by what feels manageable and appropriate) to your class. Children will then read this same section, using your modelled intonation and expression. They will need to track the text in front of them, actively participating in the 'reading' of the text, rather than passively listening to you as you read the text. This is key to supporting their improving automaticity.

Delivery step 2:

You can then read the text again in larger chunks. Children will again echo these chunks back to you. On this read you will model this same expression and intonation but also model reading smoothly and with an appropriate pace.

Delivery step 3:

This will be where you model the expression and intonation appropriate to the text type.

Read the whole text to your class or group. Ensure you are modelling expressive reading and are observing your pace and punctuation. This will support their understanding of *how* to read fluently. Then, working with a partner, children can practise reading the whole text expressively to each other.

Optional follow-up steps:

Some children may further benefit from small groups where repeated reading of the Anthology text takes place. Other children may further benefit from reading the Anthology texts 1:1.

ELS Fluency must be used in conjunction with your ELS assessment processes to ensure that children are only being asked to read texts that are six weeks behind their current phonic knowledge. Children cannot read an ELS Fluency text that contains GPCs that they do not know. Fluency requires existing knowledge of the graphemes alongside repeated practice to allow 'fluent' application.

SEND learners

ELS Fluency can be used with all pupils once they have completed the teaching of the linked content 6 weeks in advance of reading the fluency texts. This means that children may complete their Fluency session at any time, and these can be conducted in smaller groups or 1:1 if appropriate. Some children may benefit from reading the texts in the Anthologies more times than is suggested in this Handbook; this can be achieved by having additional sessions to read the text before moving on. Some children may need the texts from the Anthologies broken down into smaller sections – this can be led by the needs of the child.

Where pupils are working with the slowed ELS progression, you may find that they benefit from reading an Anthology text over a two-week period, giving them additional practice of the previously learned graphemes.

The Elements of Fluency

Accuracy

When thinking about accuracy, we consider the pronunciation of the words within the text alongside the accurate reading of the words. This means that children will recognize the sound-to-spelling correspondences to be able to read each word correctly. If they have pre-read the progress check, they should have identified which is the correct pronunciation of the word and applied this when reading for the second time.

Automaticity

When we describe children as reading with automaticity, we mean that they are decoding without overt sounding and blending. Automatic reading means recognizing almost all the words encountered within texts. Where words are unknown, the reader is able to use their secure GPC knowledge to decode these words without overt sounding and blending.

Expression

We describe the reading of texts with stress, expression and intonation that is appropriate to the text-type as prosodic. This is what we are listening for. Has the child read the text with expression and intonation? Does it sound interesting to listen to? Have they used the correct expression for the text-type?

To read with prosody that is appropriate for the text, children will need to have understood the text-type.

Vocabulary and Language Knowledge

To read with prosody, some, if not all children will need to have understood the language and vocabulary within the text. This understanding will support their phrasing, expression, stress and intonation. The simple questions following the text will help to further identify a child's understanding of what they have read. Knowledge of the language and vocabulary will also support meaning activation and accuracy for pronunciation. This means that, for children who have a command of the language within the text, the reading of the text will sound more prosodic, smoother and more accurate.

During fluency sessions, give and explain the meaning of new words or ideas and phrases to allow for all children to access the vocabulary and language within the text. This is built on the same principles used in your ELS lessons.

Modelled and repeated reading

During your fluency sessions you will model reading texts to the children and encourage repeated reading, through re-reading the fluency texts in the Anthologies but also by re-reading decodable texts from earlier on in the phonics programme.

Modelled reading is the key to demonstrating *how* to read with prosody. This is a core element of ELS Fluency. Children should be able to mimic your expression but also develop their own prosody through understanding the text-type, the appropriate phrasing and being given the chance to re-read the texts they are presented with.

Vocabulary and language knowledge should continue to be supported to ensure that all children have the same access.

readerful

Fluency and Readerful

Readerful and the Readerful Fluency Checks are the perfect next step after ELS for children to continue their fluency journey.

Readerful is a rich, linked library of inclusive books, providing a flexible whole-school reading spine of the best books for reading aloud and independent reading. These are accompanied by easy-to-use expert teaching support, which includes fluency CPD and the Readerful Fluency Checks (for Year 2/P3 to Year 6/P7). Readerful's strategies for fluency success, including explicit teaching, building reading miles and checking fluency where needed, are an ideal follow-on after the completion of the ELS Fluency programme.

To find out more about Readerful, visit http://www.oxfordprimary.com/readerful

To book a reading review with an Oxford Educational Consultant, or to discover more ways ELS can help young readers, email primary.enquiries@oup.com and one of the team will be in touch to book an appointment.

ELS Fluency Progression

Year One / P2

Week of Teaching	Essential Letters and Sounds Content	Matched Fluency text content *	Matched Fluency text title
Y1 / P2 **Aut 1 Week 1**	Review Y1:1	CVCC –ed /ed/	*Anthology 1*: A Card for Nan
Y1 / P2 **Aut 1 Week 2**	Review Y1:2	CCVC –ed /t/	*Anthology 1*: The Big Brown Slug
Y1 / P2 **Aut 1 Week 3**	/ai/ <ay>, /ow/ <ou>, /igh/ <ie>, /ee/ <ea>	CCVCC –ed /d/	*Anthology 1*: Lunch for Dad
Y1 / P2 **Aut 1 Week 4**	/oi/ <oy>, /ur/ <ir>, /(y)oo/ <ue>, /or/ <aw>	CCCVC	*Anthology 1*: Squirrels
Y1 / P2 **Aut 1 Week 5**	Review Y1:3	Review	*Anthology 1*: Camping
Y1 / P2 **Aut 1 Week 6**	/w/ <wh>, /f/ <ph>, /(y)oo/ <ew>, /oa/ <oe>	CCCVCC	*Anthology 1*: On the Swings
Y1 / P2 **Aut 2 Week 1**	/or/ <au>, /ee/ <ey>, /ai/ <a–e>, /ee/ <e–e>	Review Y1:1	*Anthology 1*: Frogs
Y1 / P2 **Aut 2 Week 2**	/igh/ <i–e>, /oa/ <o–e>, /(y)oo/ <u–e>, /s/ <c>	Review Y1:2	*Anthology 1*: Snow
Y1 / P2 **Aut 2 Week 3**	/ee/ <y>, /or/ <al> Review Y1:4	/ai/ <ay>, /ow/ <ou>, /igh/ <ie>, /ee/ <ea>	*Anthology 1*: The Pie Contest
Y1 / P2 **Aut 2 Week 4**	Review Y1:5	/oi/ <oy>, /ur/ <ir>, /(y)oo/ <ue>, /or/ <aw>	*Anthology 1*: Bird Feeders
Y1 / P2 **Aut 2 Week 5**	Review Y1:6	Review Y1:3	*Anthology 1*: Beach Creatures
Y1 / P2 **Aut 2 Week 6**	Review Y1:7	/w/ <wh>, /f/ <ph>, /(y)oo/ <ew>, /oa/ <oe>	*Anthology 1*: Spotting Dolphins
Y1 / P2 **Spr 1 Week 1**	Review Y1:8	/or/ <au>, /ee/ <ey>, /ai/ <a–e>, /ee/ <e–e>	*Anthology 1*: Stay Safe at the Beach
Y1 / P2 **Spr 1 Week 2**	/ai/ <a>, /ai/ <ey>, /ai/ <ea>, /ai/ <eigh>, /ar/ <a>, /ee/ <e>, /igh/ <i> /igh/ <y>	/igh/ <i–e>, /oa/ <o–e>, /(y)oo/ <u–e>, /s/ <c>	*Anthology 1*: The Amusement Park
Y1 / P2 **Spr 1 Week 3**	/oa/ <o>, /o/ <a>, /oo/ <u>, /y/+/oo/ <u>, /c/ <ch>, /sh/ <ch>, /e/ <ea>	/ee/ <y> /or/ <al> Review Y1:4	*Anthology 1*: Go Outside

Week of Teaching	Essential Letters and Sounds Content	Matched Fluency text content *	Matched Fluency text title
Y1 / P2 **Spr 1 Week 4**	/ur/ <or>, /ur/ <ear>, /oo/ <ou>, /oa/+/l/ <oul>, /ee/ <ie>, /v/ <ve>, /i/ <y>	Review Y1:5	*Anthology 1*: The Missing Spaceship Part
Y1 / P2 **Spr 1 Week 5**	Review Y1:9	Review Y1:6	*Anthology 1*: Scout
Y1 / P2 **Spr 1 Week 6**	/air/ <are>, /air/ <ere>, /air/ <ear>, /ch/ <tch>	Review Y1:7	*Anthology 1*: Dawn
Y1 / P2 **Spr 2 Week 1**	/u/ <o>, Review Y1:10	Review Y1:8	*Anthology 1*: Ice Hockey
Y1 / P2 **Spr 2 Week 2**	/j/ <g>, /j/ <ge>, /j/ <dge>, /s/ <st>	/ai/ <a>, /ai/ <ey>, /ai/ <ea>, /ai/ <eigh>, /ar/ <a>, /ee/ <e>, /igh/ <i>, /igh/ <y>	*Anthology 1*: Queen of the Forest
Y1 / P2 **Spr 2 Week 3**	/s/ <ce>, /s/ <se>, /n/ <gn>, /n/ <kn>, /r/ <wr>, /m/ <mb>	/oa/ <o>, /o/ <a>, /oo/ <u>, /y/+/oo/ <u>, /c/ <ch>, /sh/ <ch>, /e/ <ea>	*Anthology 1*: Schools of the Future
Y1 / P2 **Spr 2 Week 4**	/z/ <se>, /z/ <ze>, /ear/ <eer>, /ear/ <ere>, /sh/ <ti>, /sh/ –tion	/ur/ <or>, /ur/<ear>, /oo/ <ou>, /oa/+/l/ <oul>, /ee/ <ie>, /v/ <ve>, /i/ <y>	*Anthology 1*: The Blackberry Mystery
Y1 / P2 **Spr 2 Week 5**	Review week Y1:11	Review Y1:9	*Anthology 1*: Chimps
Y1 / P2 **Spr 2 Week 6**	/ar/ <al>, /or/ <augh>, /sh/ <ss>, /zh/ <si>, /sh/ <ti> (–tious), /sh/ <ci> (–ous, –ion, –ian)	/air/ <are>, /air/ <ere>, /air/ <ear>, /ch/ <tch>	*Anthology 1*: Nightmare or Dream?
Y1 / P2 **Sum 1 Week 1**	Review	/u/ <o>, Review Y1:10	*Anthology 1*: Leaf Art
Y1 / P2 **Sum 1 Week 2**	Review	/j/ <g>, /j/ <ge>, /j/ <dge>, /s/ <st>	*Anthology 1*: Pearls
Y1 / P2 **Sum 1 Week 3**	Review	/s/ <ce>, /s/ <se>, /n/ <gn>, /n/ <kn>, /r/ <wr>, /m/ <mb>	*Anthology 1*: Forest school fun
Y1 / P2 **Sum 1 Week 4**	Review	/z/ <se>, /z/ <ze>, /ear/ <eer>, /ear/ <ere>, /sh/ <ti>, /sh/ <ti> –tion	*Anthology 1*: Dogs can Help
Y1 / P2 **Sum 1 Week 5**	Review	Review Y1:11	*Anthology 1*: Rehome a Toy
Y1 / P2 **Sum 1 Week 6**	Review	/ar/ <al>, /or/ <augh>, /sh/ <ss>, /zh/ <si>, /sh/ <ti> (–tious), /sh/ <ci> (–ous, –ion, –ian)	*Anthology 1*: Buttercup is Missing!
Y1 / P2 **Sum 2 Week 1**	/s/ <sc>, /n/ <ne>, /g/ <gh>, /g/ <gu>	Review	*Anthology 1*: Woolly Hats

Week of Teaching	Essential Letters and Sounds Content	Matched Fluency text content *	Matched Fluency text title
Y1 / P2 **Sum 2 Week 2**	/u/ <ou>, /f/ <gh>, /o/ <ou>, /u/ <oo>	Review	*Anthology 1*: West Green Football Team Needs a Goalkeeper
Y1 / P2 **Sum 2 Week 3**	/oo/ <o>, /h/ <wh>, /w/ <u>, /ee/ <ei>	Review	*Anthology 1*: Under a Rock
Y1 / P2 **Sum 2 Week 4**	/ee/ <i>, /oa/ <ough>, /ur/ <our>, /ur/ <re>	Review	*Anthology 1*: Bulldozer
Y1 / P2 **Sum 2 Week 5**	Review	Review	*Anthology 1*: Happy Honey!
Y1 / P2 **Sum 2 Week 6**	/t/ <te>, /or/ <ar>, /oar/ <oor>	Review	*Anthology 1*: My Brother the Super-Toddler!

Year Two / P3

Week of Teaching	ELS Essential Spelling content	Matched Fluency text content *	Matched Fluency text title
Y2 / P3 **Aut 1 Week 1**	Spellings of /ai/ Spellings of /ee/	/s/ <sc>, /n/ <ne>, /g/ <gh>, /g/ <gu>	*Anthology 2*: A Guide to the Moon
Y2 / P3 **Aut 1 Week 2**	Spellings of /igh/ Spellings of /oa/ Spellings of /(y)oo/	/u/ <ou>, /f/ <gh>, /o/ <ou>, /u/ <oo>	*Anthology 2*: Double Trouble
Y2 / P3 **Aut 1 Week 3**	/j/ spelled <g> /j/ spelled <ge> /j/ spelled <dge>	/oo/ <o>, /h/ <wh>, /w/ <u>, /ee/ <ei>	*Anthology 2*: A Trip to the Zoo
Y2 / P3 **Aut 1 Week 4**	/n/ spelled <kn> /n/ spelled <gn> /r/ spelled <wr>	/ee/ <i>, /oa/ <ough>, /ur/ <our>, /ur/ <re>	*Anthology 2*: A Journey to Italy
Y2 / P3 **Aut 1 Week 5**	/ee/ spelled <ey> /s/ spelled <c> /l/ spelled <il>	Review	*Anthology 2*: The Monster Feast
Y2 / P3 **Aut 1 Week 6**	/or/ spelled <oor> Common words: because, most /igh/ spelled <i>	/t/ <te>, /or/ <ar>, <oar> <oor>	*Anthology 2*: Animal Hoarders
Y2 / P3 **Aut 1 Week 7**	/u/ spelled <o> /o/ spelled <a> /or/ spelled <a>/<al>	Review	*Anthology 2*: A Trip to London

Week of Teaching	ELS Essential Spelling content	Matched Fluency text content *	Matched Fluency text title
Y2 / P3 **Aut 2 Week 1**	/zh/ spelled <s> /zh/ spelled <si>	Spellings of /ai/ Spellings of /ee/	*Anthology 2*: Honey
Y2 / P3 **Aut 2 Week 2**	/ur/ spelled <or> /or/ spelled <ar>	Spellings of /igh/ Spellings of /oa/ Spellings of /(y)oo/	*Anthology 2*: The Snowstorm
Y2 / P3 **Aut 2 Week 3**	/j/ spelled <g> /n/ spelled <gn> /s/ spelled <c>	/j/ spelled <g> /j/ spelled <ge> /j/ spelled <dge>	*Anthology 2*: Roger the Explorer
Y2 / P3 **Aut 2 Week 4**	/j/ spelled <ge> /n/ spelled <kn> /ee/ spelled <ey>	/n/ spelled <kn> /n/ spelled <gn> /r/ spelled <wr>	*Anthology 2*: The Knitted Gnomes
Y2 / P3 **Aut 2 Week 5**	/u/ spelled <o> /zh/ spelled <s> or <si> /r/ spelled <wr>	/ee/ spelled <ey> /s/ spelled <c> /l/ spelled <il>	*Anthology 2*: Our Beach Day
Y2 / P3 **Aut 2 Week 6**	/oo/ spelled <o> /h/ spelled <wh> /ai/ spelled <ea>	/or/ spelled <oor> Common words: because, most /igh/ spelled <i>	*Anthology 2*: Tigers
Y2 / P3 **Aut 2 Week 7**	/j/ spelled <dge> /o/ spelled <a> /or/ spelled <a>/<al>	/u/ spelled <o> /o/ spelled <a> /or/ spelled <a>/<al>	*Anthology 2*: Big Ben
Y2 / P3 **Spr 1 Week 1**	/l/ spelled <el> /l/ spelled <le> /l/ spelled <al>	/zh/ spelled <s> /zh/ spelled <si>	*Anthology 2*: The Quiet Firework Display
Y2 / P3 **Spr 1 Week 2**	doubling consonants of CVC words when adding a suffix –ed	/ur/ spelled <or> /or/ spelled <ar>	*Anthology 2*: Sensational Starfish
Y2 / P3 **Spr 1 Week 3**	doubling consonants of CVC words when adding a suffix –er	/j/ spelled <g> /n/ spelled <gn> /s/ spelled <c>	*Anthology 2*: The Big Race
Y2 / P3 **Spr 1 Week 4**	doubling consonants of CVC words when adding a suffix –y, –est and –ing	/j/ spelled <ge> /n/ spelled <kn> /ee/ spelled <ey>	*Anthology 2*: The New-Old Park

Week of Teaching	**ELS Essential Spelling content**	**Matched Fluency text content ***	**Matched Fluency text title**
Y2 / P3 **Spr 1 Week 5**	Homophones	/u/ spelled <o> /zh/ spelled <s> or <si> /r/ spelled <wr>	*Anthology 2*: The School Play
Y2 / P3 **Spr 1 Week 6**	/oa/ spelled <o> /e/ and /ee/ spelled <e> /oa/ spelled <o>	/oo/ spelled <o> /h/ spelled <wh> /ai/ spelled <ea>	*Anthology 2*: Match Report
Y2 / P3 **Spr 2 Week 1**	Apostrophes	/l/ spelled <el> /l/ spelled <le> /l/ spelled <al>	*Anthology 2*: Super Skeleton
Y2 / P3 **Spr 2 Week 2**	drop <e> and add suffix –ing	doubling consonants of CVC words when adding a suffix –ed	*Anthology 2*: The Knitting Needles
Y2 / P3 **Spr 2 Week 3**	drop <e> and add suffix –ed (–ed /ed/)	doubling consonants of CVC words when adding a suffix –er	*Anthology 2*: Playing the Drums
Y2 / P3 **Spr 2 Week 4**	drop <e> and add suffix –er	doubling consonants of CVC words when adding a suffix –y, –est and –ing	*Anthology 2*: Training Scruffy
Y2 / P3 **Spr 2 Week 5**	drop <e> and add suffix: –y, –est /ar/ spelled <a> and other CEWs	Homophones	*Anthology 2*: Walk the Plank!
Y2 / P3 **Spr 2 Week 6**	Common words: people, busy, water, would, should, could /oo/ spelled <oul> –tion endings	/oa/ spelled <o> /e/ and /ee/ spelled <e> /oa/ spelled <o>	*Anthology 2*: Violet's Boot
Y2 / P3 **Sum 1 Week 1**	Suffix –ment with no change to the root word	Apostrophes	*Anthology 2*: Jack's Mum's Eggs
Y2 / P3 **Sum 1 Week 2**	Suffix –ly with no change to the root word	drop <e> and add suffix –ing	*Anthology 2*: Snow Day
Y2 / P3 **Sum 1 Week 3**	Suffix –ful with no change to the root word	drop <e> and add suffix –ed (–ed /ed/)	*Anthology 2*: Dev's Dance
Y2 / P3 **Sum 1 Week 4**	Suffix –less with no change to the root word	drop <e> and add suffix –er	*Anthology 2*: The Deep

Week of Teaching	ELS Essential Spelling content	Matched Fluency text content *	Matched Fluency text title
Y2 / P3 **Sum 1 Week 5**	Adding –ly after another suffix (ful/less)	drop <e> and add suffix: –y, –est <a> spelled /ar/ and other CEWs	*Anthology 2*: Whales
Y2 / P3 **Sum 1 Week 6**	Suffix –ness with no change to the root word	Common words: people, busy, water, would, should, could /oo/ spelled <oul> –tion endings	*Anthology 2*: Volcanoes
Y2 / P3 **Sum 2 Week 1**	Drop the <y>, add an <i>. Add –ed where <y> is spelling /igh/ and /ee/	Suffix –ment with no change to the root word	*Anthology 2*: The Broken Bell
Y2 / P3 **Sum 2 Week 2**	Drop the <y>, add an <i>. Add –es where <y> is spelling /igh/ and /ee/	Suffix –ly with no change to the root word	*Anthology 2*: Fran's Bright Night
Y2 / P3 **Sum 2 Week 3**	Comparatives and superlatives Drop the <y>, add an<i>, add –er and –est	Suffix –ful with no change to the root word	*Anthology 2*: Gran's Mixed-up Meals
Y2 / P3 **Sum 2 Week 4**	Where root word has a doubled consonant and added <y>, drop the <y>, add an <i>, add –er and –est	Suffix –less with no change to the root word	*Anthology 2*: The Lost Locket
Y2 / P3 **Sum 2 Week 5**	Common words: sugar, eye, again, any, many, beautiful, hour, parents, sure, clothes	Adding –ly after another suffix (ful/less)	*Anthology 2*: Aunt May's Dish
Y2 / P3 **Sum 2 Week 6**	Review	Suffix –ness with no change to the root word	*Anthology 2*: A New Sister
Y2 / P3 **Sum 2 Week 7**	Review	Review	*Anthology 2*: Amazing Cats

**Children's fluency text should feature code that is one half term earlier than their current phonic knowledge. This means that if children have gaps in their GPC knowledge, you will need to determine which week of ELS Fluency they should be reading.*

ELS Fluency Progress Checks

The rest of this Handbook provides the instructions and content needed for all of the half-termly ELS Fluency progress checks.

Progress checks will take place in Week 5 of every half term in Y1/P2 and Y2/P3. The checks will support you to determine how to ensure all children are developing their fluent application of the secure GPC knowledge.

The Fluency progress checks are based around short passages of text. These texts match to the previously rehearsed content. The progress checks determine how fluently your children are reading the texts.

There is guidance overleaf from each progress check form determine next steps for you both in whole-class and 1:1 situations. Note that the guidance following the assessment can only be applied if you are accurately using the fluency checks in-line with children's current phonic knowledge (see page 8).

Progress checks: assessment and next steps

Year One/P2

You can use the A, B or C gradings which sit alongside each progress check to help determine which area requires further development. Where the child requires support with an area you can use the guidance below to identify their next steps. These areas of focus are still developing across this academic year and therefore you should consider how each child's reading of the text compares to their peers as well as these gradings.

- It may be that compared to their peers a child needs further support in a specific area. This would require 1:1 support.
- It may be that the whole class needs support with one area of focus. In this case, you can ensure that this is targeted across the next half term.

These progress checks include one question for the children to answer after reading the text for the second time. The focus here is whether they have understood the text without there being the need for arduous searching for the answer within the text. They can look for the answer, but it should be a quick check rather than an extended search. For example, the first text is about a child looking for bowls. This is the purpose of the text. If the child cannot easily recall what the child was doing in the text without looking – have they really understood?

Year Two/P3

These progress checks include the same A, B or C gradings. In the second year of ELS Fluency these gradings will support you to determine with accuracy the ways in which a child can become a more fluent reader. These areas, where identified, should have targeted support during 1:1 reading sessions, reading lessons and ELS Fluency sessions.

The questions that follow the second reading of the texts are designed to demonstrate understanding and that they know how to find the answer within the texts. This supports your overall understanding of each child as a reader and their progress towards to curriculum outcomes for Key Stage 1.

Overview of the Progress Check pages

Below is an example Progress Check with key features indicated. All the Progress Checks are structured in the same way, though there are differences in the assessment and follow-up advice.

Instructions on how to conduct this Progress Check →

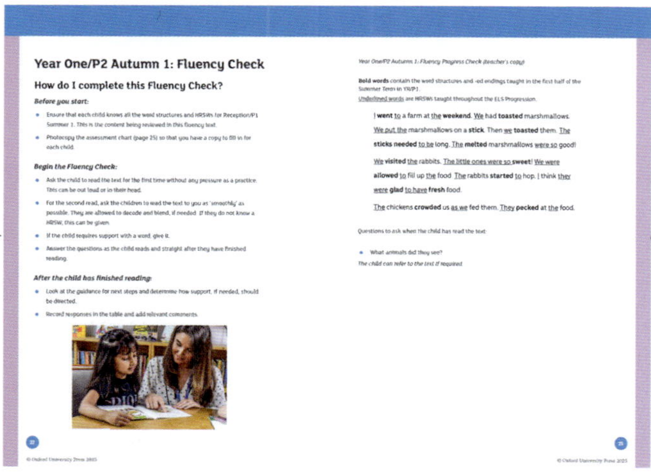
Year One/P2 Autumn 1: Fluency Check

How do I complete this Fluency Check?

← Teacher's version of the Progress Check text, with recent GPCs and HRSWs indicated

Questions and scales to help you assess each child's fluency during their read of the Progress Check text →

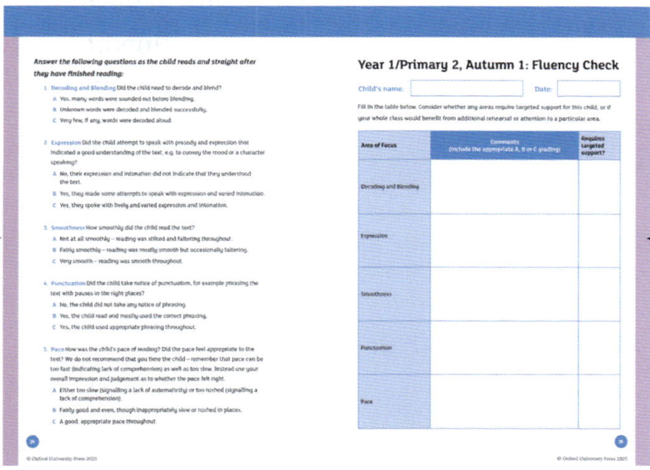
Year 1/Primary 2, Autumn 1: Fluency Check

← Photocopiable table to record the results of the Progress Check

Advice on next steps is provided, which you can consult after considering the results of the Progress Check →

I went to a farm at the weekend. We had toasted marshmallows. We put the marshmallows on a stick. Then we toasted them. The sticks needed to be long. The melted marshmallows were so good!

We visited the rabbits. The little ones were so sweet! We were allowed to fill up the food. The rabbits started to hop. I think they were glad to have fresh food.

The chickens crowded us as we fed them. They pecked at the food.

← Child's version of the Progress Check text – children should be given this version to read from

Reception Summer 2: Optional Fluency Check

How do I complete this Fluency Check?

Before you start:

- Ensure that each child knows all the GPCs and HRSWs for Reception/P1 Spring 1. This is the content being reviewed in this fluency text.
- Photocopy the assessment chart (page 19) so that you have a copy to fill in for each child.

Begin the Fluency Check:

- Ask the child to read the text for the first time without any pressure as a practice. This can be out loud or in their head.
- For the second read, ask the children to read the text to you as 'smoothly' as possible. They are allowed to decode and blend, if needed. If they do not know a HRSW, this can be given.
- If the child requires support with a word, give it.
- Answer the questions as the child reads and straight after they have finished reading.

After the child has finished reading:

- Look at the guidance for next steps and determine how support, if needed, should be directed.
- Record responses in the table and add relevant comments.

Reception/P1 Summer 2: Optional Fluency Progress Check (teacher's copy)

Bold words contain GPCs taught in the Spring Term of YR/P1.
Underlined words are the HRSWs taught throughout the ELS Progression.

We set up **for** lunch. We all had a job. It was my job to get the **bowls**.

I went to **look for** the **bowls**. My dad had put them all on the shelf. I got my **stool**. I **stood** on my **stool** and got the **bowls down**. I **took** them to my dad.

Dad held the **bowls near** the pot. He put **food** in them. Then Dad **took** the **bowls** to my mum. Mum said thank you.

Questions to ask when the child has read the text:

- What was the child getting from the shelf?

The child can refer to the text if required.

Answer the following questions as the child reads and straight after they have finished reading:

1. **Decoding and Blending** Did the child need to decode and blend?

   A Yes, many words were sounded out before blending.

   B Unknown words were decoded and blended successfully.

   C Very few, if any, words were decoded aloud.

2. **Expression** Did the child attempt to speak with prosody and expression that indicated a good understanding of the text, e.g. to convey the mood or a character speaking?

   A No, their expression and intonation did not indicate that they understood the text.

   B Yes, they made some attempts to speak with expression and varied intonation.

   C Yes, they spoke with lively and varied expression and intonation.

3. **Smoothness** How smoothly did the child read the text?

   A Not at all smoothly – reading was stilted and faltering throughout.

   B Fairly smoothly – reading was mostly smooth but occasionally faltering.

   C Very smooth – reading was smooth throughout.

4. **Punctuation** Did the child take notice of punctuation, for example phrasing the text with pauses in the right places?

   A No, the child did not take any notice of phrasing.

   B Yes, the child read and mostly used the correct phrasing.

   C Yes, the child used appropriate phrasing throughout.

5. **Pace** How was the child's pace of reading? Did the pace feel appropriate to the text? We do not recommend that you time the child – remember that pace can be too fast (indicating lack of comprehension) as well as too slow. Instead use your overall impression and judgement as to whether the pace felt right.

   A Either too slow (signalling a lack of automaticity) or too rushed (signalling a lack of comprehension).

   B Fairly good and even, though inappropriately slow or rushed in places.

   C A good, appropriate pace throughout.

Reception Summer 2: Optional Fluency Check

Child's name: ______________ **Date:** ______________

Fill in the table below. Consider whether any areas require targeted support for this child, or if your whole class would benefit from additional rehearsal or attention to a particular area.

Area of Focus	Comments	Requires support (see page 20)
Decoding and Blending (this is the most important thing to target with more practice of blending words that they already know)		
Punctuation		
Expression Smoothness Pace	*If children are actively engaged in decoding and blending, it is likely they will score A or B for these categories. This may not be because they don't know the GPCs, but may be because they have not read enough words that contain those GPCs. Further practice of reading texts that contain known GPCs will help to support this.*	

Guidance when deciding on next steps:

Decoding and Blending – ensure that the child reads a wider range of texts matched to their secure and current phonic knowledge to allow for application of their understanding. These should offer a wide range of vocabulary and language to ensure that children are developing their orthographic map. Children can re-read texts from earlier in the programme as well as read multiple texts from the same week to widen their application of their GPC knowledge.

For this assessment, further practice of these GPCs can be found in Essential Phonic Readers Reception Spring 1:

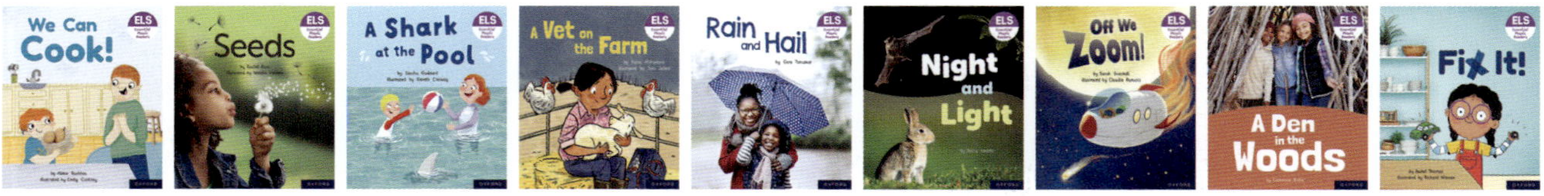

Punctuation – ensure that punctuation is explained and its impact on reading is modelled.

Expression – use the weekly fluency texts and texts matched to the week of teaching to model reading with expression and intonation. Where appropriate, use echo or choral reading techniques to develop understanding of *how* to read a text with prosody.

To support both decoding and blending *and* prosody, ensure that you make full use of the Essential Phonic Readers and Essential Blending Books that accompany Essential Letters and Sounds. These texts can be used both alongside current phonic knowledge as well as to develop fluent application of known GPCs. These books from Essential Phonic Readers Reception Spring 2 can be used:

Smoothness – additional practice of re-reading texts that use secure code knowledge. When assigning texts for home reading matched to current phonic knowledge for rehearsal, include a 'fluency' text that contains secure code knowledge. We recommend that children take home a book that is six weeks behind their 'current' knowledge book.

Pace – this should be modelled during all teacher-led reading. Re-reading texts will allow children to develop their reading at an appropriate pace as they become familiar with the text and its content.

There are many factors that can affect a child's reading on any one day. If a child's Fluency Check results don't reflect your knowledge of the child, consider running the check again using the alternative extract or a book at the same level, and use your own judgement when deciding which next steps to follow. The Fluency Check gives you a means of gaining additional information about a child's reading which you can use alongside everything else you know.

If children are not recognising the GPCs that they know in the text, they may require additional support with blending for reading. For this, you can use the ELS Blending for Reading Intervention.

We set up for lunch. We all had a job. It was my job to get the bowls.

I went to look for the bowls. My dad had put them all on the shelf. I got my stool. I stood on my stool and got the bowls down. I took them to my dad.

Dad held the bowls near the pot. He put food in them. Then Dad took the bowls to my mum. Mum said thank you.

Year One/P2 Autumn 1: Fluency Check

How do I complete this Fluency Check?

Before you start:

- Ensure that each child knows all the word structures and HRSWs for Reception/P1 Summer 1. This is the content being reviewed in this fluency text.
- Photocopy the assessment chart (page 25) so that you have a copy to fill in for each child.

Begin the Fluency Check:

- Ask the child to read the text for the first time without any pressure as a practice. This can be out loud or in their head.
- For the second read, ask the children to read the text to you as 'smoothly' as possible. They are allowed to decode and blend, if needed. If they do not know a HRSW, this can be given.
- If the child requires support with a word, give it.
- Answer the questions as the child reads and straight after they have finished reading.

After the child has finished reading:

- Look at the guidance for next steps and determine how support, if needed, should be directed.
- Record responses in the table and add relevant comments.

Year One/P2 Autumn 1: Fluency Progress Check (teacher's copy)

Bold words contain the word structures and -ed endings taught in the first half of the Summer Term in YR/P1.

Underlined words are HRSWs taught throughout the ELS Progression.

I **went** to a farm at the **weekend**. We had **toasted** marshmallows. We put the marshmallows on a **stick**. Then we **toasted** them. The **sticks needed** to be long. The **melted** marshmallows were so good!

We **visited** the rabbits. The little ones were so **sweet**! We were **allowed** to fill up the food. The rabbits **started** to hop. I think they were **glad** to have **fresh** food.

The chickens **crowded** us as we fed them. They **pecked** at the food.

Questions to ask when the child has read the text:

- What animals did they see?

The child can refer to the text if required.

Answer the following questions as the child reads and straight after they have finished reading:

1. **Decoding and Blending** Did the child need to decode and blend?
   - **A** Yes, many words were sounded out before blending.
   - **B** Unknown words were decoded and blended successfully.
   - **C** Very few, if any, words were decoded aloud.

2. **Expression** Did the child attempt to speak with prosody and expression that indicated a good understanding of the text, e.g. to convey the mood or a character speaking?
   - **A** No, their expression and intonation did not indicate that they understood the text.
   - **B** Yes, they made some attempts to speak with expression and varied intonation.
   - **C** Yes, they spoke with lively and varied expression and intonation.

3. **Smoothness** How smoothly did the child read the text?
   - **A** Not at all smoothly – reading was stilted and faltering throughout.
   - **B** Fairly smoothly – reading was mostly smooth but occasionally faltering.
   - **C** Very smooth – reading was smooth throughout.

4. **Punctuation** Did the child take notice of punctuation, for example phrasing the text with pauses in the right places?
   - **A** No, the child did not take any notice of phrasing.
   - **B** Yes, the child read and mostly used the correct phrasing.
   - **C** Yes, the child used appropriate phrasing throughout.

5. **Pace** How was the child's pace of reading? Did the pace feel appropriate to the text? We do not recommend that you time the child – remember that pace can be too fast (indicating lack of comprehension) as well as too slow. Instead use your overall impression and judgement as to whether the pace felt right.
   - **A** Either too slow (signalling a lack of automaticity) or too rushed (signalling a lack of comprehension).
   - **B** Fairly good and even, though inappropriately slow or rushed in places.
   - **C** A good, appropriate pace throughout.

Year 1/Primary 2, Autumn 1: Fluency Check

Child's name: ______________________ **Date:** ______________

Fill in the table below. Consider whether any areas require targeted support for this child, or if your whole class would benefit from additional rehearsal or attention to a particular area.

Area of Focus	Comments (include the appropriate A, B or C grading)	Requires targeted support?
Decoding and Blending		
Expression		
Smoothness		
Punctuation		
Pace		

Guidance when deciding on next steps:

Decoding and Blending – ensure that the child reads a wider range of texts matched to their secure and current phonic knowledge are used to allow for application of their understanding. These should offer a wide range of vocabulary and language to ensure that children are developing their orthographic map. Children can re-read texts from earlier in the programme as well as read multiple texts from the same week to widen their application of their GPC knowledge.

For this assessment, further practice of these GPCs can be found in Essential Phonic Readers Reception Summer 1 and 2:

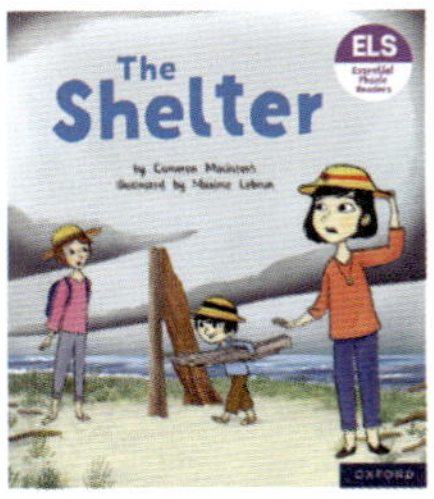

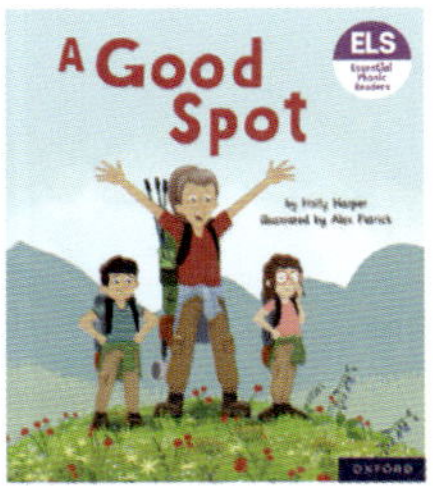

Expression – use the weekly fluency texts and texts matched to the week of teaching to model reading with expression and intonation. Where appropriate, use echo or choral reading techniques to develop understanding of *how* to read a text with prosody.

Smoothness – additional practice of re-reading texts that use secure code knowledge. When assigning texts for home reading matched to current phonic knowledge for rehearsal, include a 'fluency' text that contains secure code knowledge. We recommend that children take home a book that is six weeks behind their 'current' knowledge book.

Punctuation – ensure that punctuation is explained and its impact on reading is modelled.

Pace – this should be modelled during all teacher-led reading. Re-reading texts will allow children to develop their reading at an appropriate pace as they become familiar with the text and its content.

There are many factors that can affect a child's reading on any one day. If a child's Fluency Check results don't reflect your knowledge of the child, consider running the check again using the alternative extract or a book at the same level, and use your own judgement when deciding which next steps to follow. The Fluency Check gives you a means of gaining additional information about a child's reading which you can use alongside everything else you know.

If children are not recognising the GPCs that they know in the text, they may require additional support with blending for reading. For this, you can use the Blending for Reading ELS Intervention.

I went to a farm at the weekend. We had toasted marshmallows. We put the marshmallows on a stick. Then we toasted them. The sticks needed to be long. The melted marshmallows were so good!

We visited the rabbits. The little ones were so sweet! We were allowed to fill up the food. The rabbits started to hop. I think they were glad to have fresh food.

The chickens crowded us as we fed them. They pecked at the food.

Year One/P2 Autumn 2: Fluency Check

How do I complete this Fluency Check?

Before you start:

- Ensure that each child knows all the GPCs and HRSWs for Year One/P2 Autumn 1. This is the content being reviewed in this fluency text.
- Photocopy the assessment chart (page 31) so that you have a copy to fill in for each child.

Begin the Fluency Check:

- Ask the child to read the text for the first time without any pressure as a practice. This can be out loud or in their head.
- For the second read, ask the children to read the text to you as 'smoothly' as possible. They are allowed to decode and blend, if needed. If they do not know a HRSW, this can be given.
- If the child requires support with a word, give it.
- Answer the questions as the child reads and straight after they have finished reading.

After the child has finished reading:

- Look at the guidance for next steps and determine how support, if needed, should be directed.
- Record responses in the table and add relevant comments.

Year One/P2 Autumn 2: Fluency Progress Check (teacher's copy)

Bold words contain GPCs taught in the first half of the Autumn Term in Y1/P2.
Underlined words are HRSWs taught throughout the ELS Progression.

The class was at Navid's house. We had a **feast**. There were sandwiches, **pies** and a **few treats**.

"Let's go and **play**!" **shouted** Navid.

Mel stood near the house. The rest of us stood at the bottom of the garden. Mel turned **around** to look at us. We stood still. Then Mel looked at the house and we crept nearer.

"Do not get spotted!" Navid's dad **shouted**.

Kim was the winner. He got nearest to the house **without** being spotted!

Questions to ask when the child has read the text:

- Have you ever played a party game?

The child can refer to the text if required.

Answer the following questions as the child reads and straight after they have finished reading:

1. **Decoding and Blending** Did the child need to decode and blend?
   - **A** Yes, many words were sounded out before blending.
   - **B** Unknown words were decoded and blended successfully.
   - **C** Very few, if any, words were decoded aloud.

2. **Expression** Did the child attempt to speak with prosody and expression that indicated a good understanding of the text, e.g. to convey the mood or a character speaking?
   - **A** No, their expression and intonation did not indicate that they understood the text.
   - **B** Yes, they made some attempts to speak with expression and varied intonation.
   - **C** Yes, they spoke with lively and varied expression and intonation.

3. **Smoothness** How smoothly did the child read the text?
   - **A** Not at all smoothly – reading was stilted and faltering throughout.
   - **B** Fairly smoothly – reading was mostly smooth but occasionally faltering.
   - **C** Very smooth – reading was smooth throughout.

4. **Punctuation** Did the child take notice of punctuation, for example phrasing the text with pauses in the right places?
   - **A** No, the child did not take any notice of phrasing.
   - **B** Yes, the child read and mostly used the correct phrasing.
   - **C** Yes, the child used appropriate phrasing throughout.

5. **Pace** How was the child's pace of reading? Did the pace feel appropriate to the text? We do not recommend that you time the child – remember that pace can be too fast (indicating lack of comprehension) as well as too slow. Instead use your overall impression and judgement as to whether the pace felt right.
   - **A** Either too slow (signalling a lack of automaticity) or too rushed (signalling a lack of comprehension).
   - **B** Fairly good and even, though inappropriately slow or rushed in places.
   - **C** A good, appropriate pace throughout.

Year 1/Primary 2, Autumn 2: Fluency Check

Child's name: ______________ **Date:** ______________

Fill in the table below. Consider whether any areas require targeted support for this child, or if your whole class would benefit from additional rehearsal or attention to a particular area.

Area of Focus	Comments (include the appropriate A, B or C grading)	Requires targeted support?
Decoding and Blending		
Expression		
Smoothness		
Punctuation		
Pace		

Guidance when deciding on next steps:

Decoding and Blending – ensure that the child reads a wider range of texts matched to their secure and current phonic knowledge to allow for application of their understanding. These should offer a wide range of vocabulary and language to ensure that children are developing their orthographic map. Children can re-read texts from earlier in the programme as well as read multiple texts from the same week to widen their application of their GPC knowledge.

For this assessment, further practice of these GPCs can be found in Essential Phonic Readers from Year One Autumn 1:

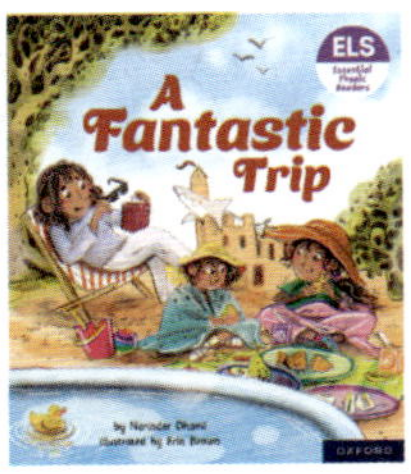

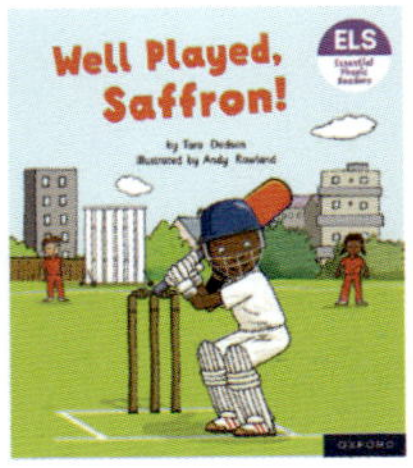

Expression – use the weekly fluency texts and texts matched to the week of teaching to model reading with expression and intonation. Where appropriate, use echo or choral reading techniques to develop understanding of *how* to read a text with prosody.

Smoothness – additional practice of re-reading texts that use secure code knowledge. When assigning texts for home read matched to current phonic knowledge for rehearsal, include a 'fluency' text that contains secure code knowledge. We recommend that children take home a book that is six weeks behind their 'current' knowledge book.

Punctuation – ensure that punctuation is explained and its impact on reading is modelled.

Pace – this should be modelled during all teacher-led reading. Re-reading texts will allow children to develop their reading at an appropriate pace as they become familiar with the text and its content.

There are many factors that can affect a child's reading on any one day. If a child's Fluency Check results don't reflect your knowledge of the child, consider running the check again using the alternative extract or a book at the same level, and use your own judgement when deciding which next steps to follow. The Fluency Check gives you a means of gaining additional information about a child's reading which you can use alongside everything else you know.

If children are not recognising the GPCs that they know in the text, they may require additional support with Blending for Reading. For this, you can use the ELS intervention.

The class was at Navid's house. We had a feast. There were sandwiches, pies and a few treats.

"Let's go and play!" shouted Navid.

Mel stood near the house. The rest of us stood at the bottom of the garden. Mel turned around to look at us. We stood still. Then Mel looked at the house and we crept nearer.

"Do not get spotted!" Navid's dad shouted.

Kim was the winner. He got nearest to the house without being spotted!

Year One/P2 Spring 1: Fluency Check

How do I complete this Fluency Check?

Before you start:

- Ensure that each child knows all the GPCs and HRSWs for Year One/P2 Autumn 2. This is the content being reviewed in this fluency text.
- Photocopy the assessment chart (page 37) so that you have a copy to fill in for each child.

Begin the Fluency Check:

- Ask the child to read the text for the first time without any pressure as a practice. This can be out loud or in their head.
- For the second read, ask the children to read the text to you as 'smoothly' as possible. They are allowed to decode and blend, if needed. If they do not know a HRSW, this can be given.
- If the child requires support with a word, give it.
- Answer the questions as the child reads and straight after they have finished reading.

After the child has finished reading:

- Look at the guidance for next steps and determine how support, if needed, should be directed.
- Record responses in the table and add relevant comments.

Year One/P2 Spring 1: Fluency Progress Check (teacher's copy)

Bold words contain GPCs taught in the second half of the Autumn Term in Y1/P2.
Underlined words are HRSWs taught throughout the ELS Progression.

We played with the dressing up outfits in the classroom.

"Come on, **Luke**. Let's dress up," I said.

Luke dressed up as a dolphin.

"Put on the cat whiskers and ears," **Mike** said to Ted.

Paul had an **ape** outfit. **Pete** and **Eve** were **mice**. Mads was a **donkey**. We **made** our own zoo!

We took the animal crew into the playground. It was so **funny**! We **walked** around and **spoke** in the sounds of the animals. We **even made funny faces**!

Questions to ask when the child has read the text:

- Name some of the animals they dressed up as?

The child can refer to the text if required.

Answer the following questions as the child reads and straight after they have finished reading:

1. **Decoding and Blending** Did the child need to decode and blend?
   - **A** Yes, many words were sounded out before blending.
   - **B** Unknown words were decoded and blended successfully.
   - **C** Very few, if any, words were decoded aloud.

2. **Expression** Did the child attempt to speak with prosody and expression that indicated a good understanding of the text, e.g. to convey the mood or a character speaking?
   - **A** No, their expression and intonation did not indicate that they understood the text.
   - **B** Yes, they made some attempts to speak with expression and varied intonation.
   - **C** Yes, they spoke with lively and varied expression and intonation.

3. **Smoothness** How smoothly did the child read the text?
   - **A** Not at all smoothly – reading was stilted and faltering throughout.
   - **B** Fairly smoothly – reading was mostly smooth but occasionally faltering.
   - **C** Very smooth – reading was smooth throughout.

4. **Punctuation** Did the child take notice of punctuation, for example phrasing the text with pauses in the right places?
   - **A** No, the child did not take any notice of phrasing.
   - **B** Yes, the child read and mostly used the correct phrasing.
   - **C** Yes, the child used appropriate phrasing throughout.

5. **Pace** How was the child's pace of reading? Did the pace feel appropriate to the text? We do not recommend that you time the child – remember that pace can be too fast (indicating lack of comprehension) as well as too slow. Instead use your overall impression and judgement as to whether the pace felt right.
   - **A** Either too slow (signalling a lack of automaticity) or too rushed (signalling a lack of comprehension).
   - **B** Fairly good and even, though inappropriately slow or rushed in places.
   - **C** A good, appropriate pace throughout.

Year 1/Primary 2, Spring 1: Fluency Check

Child's name: **Date:**

Fill in the table below. Consider whether any areas require targeted support for this child, or if your whole class would benefit from additional rehearsal or attention to a particular area.

Area of Focus	Comments (include the appropriate A, B or C grading)	Requires targeted support?
Decoding and Blending		
Expression		
Smoothness		
Punctuation		
Pace		

Guidance when deciding on next steps:

Decoding and Blending – ensure that the child reads a wider range of texts matched to their secure and current phonic knowledge to allow for application of their understanding. These should offer a wide range of vocabulary and language to ensure that children are developing their orthographic map. Children can re-read texts from earlier in the programme as well as read multiple texts from the same week to widen their application of their GPC knowledge.

For this assessment, further practice of these GPCs can be found in Essential Phonic Readers from Year One Autumn 2:

Expression – use the weekly fluency texts and texts matched to the week of teaching to model reading with expression and intonation. Where appropriate, use echo or choral reading techniques to develop understanding of *how* to read a text with prosody.

Smoothness – additional practice of re-reading texts that use secure code knowledge. When assigning texts for home reading matched to current phonic knowledge for rehearsal, include a 'fluency' text that contains secure code knowledge. We recommend that children take home a book that is six weeks behind their 'current' knowledge book.

Punctuation – ensure that punctuation is explained and its impact on reading is modelled.

Pace – this should be modelled during all teacher-led reading. Re-reading texts will allow children to develop their reading at an appropriate pace as they become familiar with the text and its content.

There are many factors that can affect a child's reading on any one day. If a child's Fluency Check results don't reflect your knowledge of the child, consider running the check again using the alternative extract or a book at the same level, and use your own judgement when deciding which next steps to follow. The Fluency Check gives you a means of gaining additional information about a child's reading which you can use alongside everything else you know.

If children are not recognising the GPCs that they know in the text, they may require additional support with Blending for Reading. For this, you can use the ELS intervention.

We played with the dressing up outfits in the classroom.

“Come on, Luke. Let’s dress up,” I said.

Luke dressed up as a dolphin.

“Put on the cat whiskers and ears,” Mike said to Ted.

Paul had an ape outfit. Pete and Eve were mice. Mads was a donkey. We made our own zoo!

We took the animal crew into the playground. It was so funny! We walked around and spoke in the sounds of the animals. We even made funny faces!

Year One/P2 Spring 2: Fluency Check

How do I complete this Fluency Check?

Before you start:

- Ensure that each child knows all the GPCs and HRSWs for Year One/P2 Spring 1. This is the content being reviewed in this fluency text.
- Photocopy the assessment chart (page 43) so that you have a copy to fill in for each child.

Begin the Fluency Check:

- Ask the child to read the text for the first time without any pressure as a practice. This can be out loud or in their head.
- For the second read, ask the children to read the text to you as 'smoothly' as possible. They are allowed to decode and blend, if needed. If they do not know a HRSW, this can be given.
- If the child requires support with a word, give it.
- Answer the questions as the child reads and straight after they have finished reading.

After the child has finished reading:

- Look at the guidance for next steps and determine how support, if needed, should be directed.
- Record responses in the table and add relevant comments.

Year One/P2 Spring 2: Fluency Progress Check (teacher's copy)

Bold words contain GPCs taught in the first half of Spring Term of Y1/P2.
Underlined words are HRSWs taught throughout the ELS Progression.

It was **sweater weather**. The **sky** was **full** of snow. The frost crunched underfoot. We were out in the **fields**. We needed to fix the **old** stone wall. One of the big **boulders** had fallen onto the **earth**.

"We must **patch** up the wall," the boss said.

"We have to be **careful** because of the **weight** of the **boulders**," I said.

We wanted to finish quickly. The **weather** was turning bad. We **only** stopped to eat some **soup** and **bread**. It was hard **work** but it was **worth** it. It looked **great**!

Questions to ask when the child has read the text:

- What were the workers fixing?

The child can refer to the text if required.

Answer the following questions as the child reads and straight after they have finished reading:

1. **Decoding and Blending** Did the child need to decode and blend?
   - **A** Yes, many words were sounded out before blending.
   - **B** Unknown words were decoded and blended successfully.
   - **C** Very few, if any, words were decoded aloud.

2. **Expression** Did the child attempt to speak with prosody and expression that indicated a good understanding of the text, e.g. to convey the mood or a character speaking?
   - **A** No, their expression and intonation did not indicate that they understood the text.
   - **B** Yes, they made some attempts to speak with expression and varied intonation.
   - **C** Yes, they spoke with lively and varied expression and intonation.

3. **Smoothness** How smoothly did the child read the text?
   - **A** Not at all smoothly – reading was stilted and faltering throughout.
   - **B** Fairly smoothly – reading was mostly smooth but occasionally faltering.
   - **C** Very smooth – reading was smooth throughout.

4. **Punctuation** Did the child take notice of punctuation, for example phrasing the text with pauses in the right places?
   - **A** No, the child did not take any notice of phrasing.
   - **B** Yes, the child read and mostly used the correct phrasing.
   - **C** Yes, the child used appropriate phrasing throughout.

5. **Pace** How was the child's pace of reading? Did the pace feel appropriate to the text? We do not recommend that you time the child – remember that pace can be too fast (indicating lack of comprehension) as well as too slow. Instead use your overall impression and judgement as to whether the pace felt right.
   - **A** Either too slow (signalling a lack of automaticity) or too rushed (signalling a lack of comprehension).
   - **B** Fairly good and even, though inappropriately slow or rushed in places.
   - **C** A good, appropriate pace throughout.

Year 1/Primary 2, Spring 2: Fluency Check

Child's name: ____________________ **Date:** ____________

Fill in the table below. Consider whether any areas require targeted support for this child, or if your whole class would benefit from additional rehearsal or attention to a particular area.

Area of Focus	Comments (include the appropriate A, B or C grading)	Requires targeted support?
Decoding and Blending		
Expression		
Smoothness		
Punctuation		
Pace		

Guidance when deciding on next steps:

Decoding and Blending – ensure that the child reads a wider range of texts matched to their secure and current phonic knowledge to allow for application of their understanding. These should offer a wide range of vocabulary and language to ensure that children are developing their orthographic map. Children can re-read texts from earlier in the programme as well as read multiple texts from the same week to widen their application of their GPC knowledge.

For this assessment, further practice of these GPCs can be found in Essential Phonic Readers from Year One Spring 1:

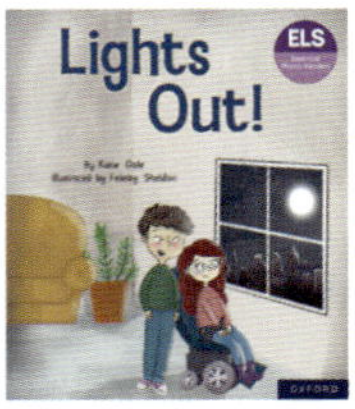

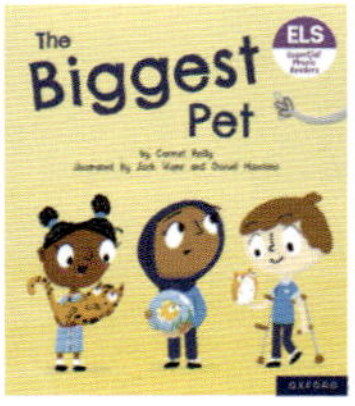

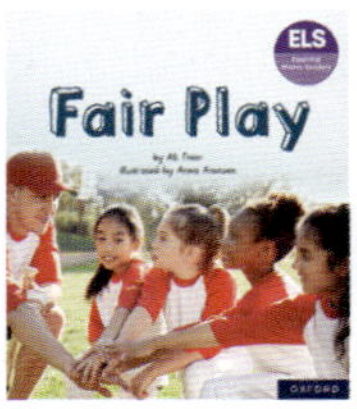

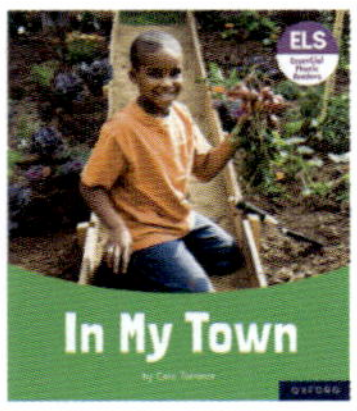

Expression – use the weekly fluency texts and texts matched to the week of teaching to model reading with expression and intonation. Where appropriate, use echo or choral reading techniques to develop understanding of *how* to read a text with prosody.

Smoothness – additional practice of re-reading texts that use secure code knowledge. When assigning texts for home read matched to current phonic knowledge for rehearsal, include a 'fluency' text that contains secure code knowledge. We recommend that children take home a book that is six weeks behind their 'current' knowledge book.

Punctuation – ensure that punctuation is explained and its impact on reading is modelled.

Pace – this should be modelled during all teacher-led reading. Re-reading texts will allow children to develop their reading at an appropriate pace as they become familiar with the text and its content.

There are many factors that can affect a child's reading on any one day. If a child's Fluency Check results don't reflect your knowledge of the child, consider running the check again using the alternative extract or a book at the same level, and use your own judgement when deciding which next steps to follow. The Fluency Check gives you a means of gaining additional information about a child's reading which you can use alongside everything else you know.

If children are not recognising the GPCs that they know in the text, they may require additional support with Blending for Reading. For this, you can use the ELS intervention.

It was sweater weather. The sky was full of snow. The frost crunched underfoot. We were out in the fields. We needed to fix the old stone wall. One of the big boulders had fallen on to the earth.

"We must patch up the wall," the boss said.

"We have to be careful because of the weight of the boulders," I said.

We wanted to finish quickly. The weather was turning bad.

We only stopped to eat some soup and bread. It was hard work but it was worth it. It looked great!

Year One/P2 Summer 1: Fluency Check

How do I complete this Fluency Check?

Before you start:

- Ensure that each child knows all the GPCs and HRSWs for Year One/P2 Spring 2. This is the content being reviewed in this fluency text.
- Photocopy the assessment chart (page 49) so that you have a copy to fill in for each child.

Begin the Fluency Check:

- Ask the child to read the text for the first time without any pressure as a practice. This can be out loud or in their head.
- For the second read, ask the children to read the text to you as 'smoothly' as possible. They are allowed to decode and blend, if needed. If they do not know a HRSW, this can be given.
- If the child requires support with a word, give it.
- Answer the questions as the child reads and straight after they have finished reading.

After the child has finished reading:

- Look at the guidance for next steps and determine how support, if needed, should be directed.
- Record responses in the table and add relevant comments.

Bold words contain GPCs taught in the second half of Spring Term in Y1/P2.
Underlined words are HRSWs taught throughout the ELS Progression.

In the summer, my **brother** got a job. It was at a very grand hotel. He was in **charge** of carrying **luggage**.

The hotel had a **large** lake with a **bridge**. There was a **large** meadow, too. There were **lambs** in it in the spring. My **brother** liked to watch the **lambs** play!

Next to the hotel, there was a wood. If you were **patient**, you could spot **deer**. They are very **cautious** animals. If you **listened** carefully, you could hear the **geese** cackle, too.

I **know** my **brother** loved his job. He has asked for a job there next summer!

Questions to ask when the child has read the text:

- Where did the brother work?

The child can refer to the text if required.

Answer the following questions as the child reads and straight after they have finished reading:

1. **Decoding and Blending** Did the child need to decode and blend?
   - **A** Yes, many words were sounded out before blending.
   - **B** Unknown words were decoded and blended successfully.
   - **C** Very few, if any, words were decoded aloud.

2. **Expression** Did the child attempt to speak with prosody and expression that indicated a good understanding of the text, e.g. to convey the mood or a character speaking?
   - **A** No, their expression and intonation did not indicate that they understood the text.
   - **B** Yes, they made some attempts to speak with expression and varied intonation.
   - **C** Yes, they spoke with lively and varied expression and intonation.

3. **Smoothness** How smoothly did the child read the text?
   - **A** Not at all smoothly – reading was stilted and faltering throughout.
   - **B** Fairly smoothly – reading was mostly smooth but occasionally faltering.
   - **C** Very smooth – reading was smooth throughout.

4. **Punctuation** Did the child take notice of punctuation, for example phrasing the text with pauses in the right places?
   - **A** No, the child did not take any notice of phrasing.
   - **B** Yes, the child read and mostly used the correct phrasing.
   - **C** Yes, the child used appropriate phrasing throughout.

5. **Pace** How was the child's pace of reading? Did the pace feel appropriate to the text? We do not recommend that you time the child – remember that pace can be too fast (indicating lack of comprehension) as well as too slow. Instead use your overall impression and judgement as to whether the pace felt right.
   - **A** Either too slow (signalling a lack of automaticity) or too rushed (signalling a lack of comprehension).
   - **B** Fairly good and even, though inappropriately slow or rushed in places.
   - **C** A good, appropriate pace throughout.

Year 1/Primary 2, Summer 1: Fluency Check

Child's name: ______________________ **Date:** ____________

Fill in the table below. Consider whether any areas require targeted support for this child, or if your whole class would benefit from additional rehearsal or attention to a particular area.

Area of Focus	Comments (include the appropriate A, B or C grading)	Requires targeted support?
Decoding and Blending		
Expression		
Smoothness		
Punctuation		
Pace		

Guidance when deciding on next steps:

Decoding and Blending – ensure that the child reads a wider range of texts matched to their secure and current phonic knowledge to allow for application of their understanding. These should offer a wide range of vocabulary and language to ensure that children are developing their orthographic map. Children can re-read texts from earlier in the programme as well as read multiple texts from the same week to widen their application of their GPC knowledge.

For this assessment, further practice of these GPCs can be found in Essential Phonic Readers from Year One Spring 2:

Expression – use the weekly fluency texts and texts matched to the week of teaching to model reading with expression and intonation. Where appropriate, use echo or choral reading techniques to develop understanding of *how* to read a text with prosody.

Smoothness – additional practice of re-reading texts that use secure code knowledge. When assigning texts for home read matched to current phonic knowledge for rehearsal, include a 'fluency' text that contains secure code knowledge. We recommend that children take home a book that is six weeks behind their 'current' knowledge book.

Punctuation – ensure that punctuation is explained and its impact on reading is modelled.

Pace – this should be modelled during all teacher-led reading. Re-reading texts will allow children to develop their reading at an appropriate pace as they become familiar with the text and its content.

There are many factors that can affect a child's reading on any one day. If a child's Fluency Check results don't reflect your knowledge of the child, consider running the check again using the alternative extract or a book at the same level, and use your own judgement when deciding which next steps to follow. The Fluency Check gives you a means of gaining additional information about a child's reading which you can use alongside everything else you know.

If children are not recognising the GPCs that they know in the text, they may require additional support with Blending for Reading. For this, you can use the ELS intervention.

In the summer, my brother got a job. It was at a very grand hotel. He was in charge of carrying luggage.

The hotel had a large lake with a bridge. There was a large meadow, too. There were lambs in it in the spring. My brother liked to watch the lambs play!

Next to the hotel, there was a wood. If you were patient, you could spot deer. They are very cautious animals. If you listened carefully, you could hear the geese cackle, too.

I know my brother loved his job. He has asked for a job there next summer!

Year One/P2 Summer 2: Fluency Check

How do I complete this Fluency Check?

Before you start:

- Ensure that each child knows all the GPCs and HRSWs for Year One/P2 Summer 1. This is the content being reviewed in this fluency text.
- Photocopy the assessment chart (page 55) so that you have a copy to fill in for each child.

Begin the Fluency Check:

- Ask the child to read the text for the first time without any pressure as a practice. This can be out loud or in their head.
- For the second read, ask the children to read the text to you as 'smoothly' as possible. They are allowed to decode and blend, if needed. If they do not know a HRSW, this can be given.
- If the child requires support with a word, give it.
- Answer the questions as the child reads and straight after they have finished reading.

After the child has finished reading:

- Look at the guidance for next steps and determine how support, if needed, should be directed.
- Record responses in the table and add relevant comments.

Underlined words are HRSWs taught throughout the ELS Progression.

The recycling plant turns old things into new things!

Engineers use special apparatus to break down objects. Then the objects can be reused. The engineers apply pressure. This squidges the items. Then they are turned into new things!

We can reuse paper, glass, plastic and metal. Recycling is good for the environment. It is good for the Earth's atmosphere, too.

We harm the Earth by cutting down trees. When we recycle, we reduce the harm we do.

Recycled glass can be used to make bottles and jars. Did you know that it can be used to make pipes and even road surfaces?

Questions to ask when the child has read the text:

- What can glass be reused to make?

The child can refer to the text if required.

Answer the following questions as the child reads and straight after they have finished reading:

1. **Decoding and Blending** Did the child need to decode and blend?
   - **A** Yes, many words were sounded out before blending.
   - **B** Unknown words were decoded and blended successfully.
   - **C** Very few, if any, words were decoded aloud.

2. **Expression** Did the child attempt to speak with prosody and expression that indicated a good understanding of the text, e.g. to convey the mood or a character speaking?
   - **A** No, their expression and intonation did not indicate that they understood the text.
   - **B** Yes, they made some attempts to speak with expression and varied intonation.
   - **C** Yes, they spoke with lively and varied expression and intonation.

3. **Smoothness** How smoothly did the child read the text?
   - **A** Not at all smoothly – reading was stilted and faltering throughout.
   - **B** Fairly smoothly – reading was mostly smooth but occasionally faltering.
   - **C** Very smooth – reading was smooth throughout.

4. **Punctuation** Did the child take notice of punctuation, for example phrasing the text with pauses in the right places?
   - **A** No, the child did not take any notice of phrasing.
   - **B** Yes, the child read and mostly used the correct phrasing.
   - **C** Yes, the child used appropriate phrasing throughout.

5. **Pace** How was the child's pace of reading? Did the pace feel appropriate to the text? We do not recommend that you time the child – remember that pace can be too fast (indicating lack of comprehension) as well as too slow. Instead use your overall impression and judgement as to whether the pace felt right.
   - **A** Either too slow (signalling a lack of automaticity) or too rushed (signalling a lack of comprehension).
   - **B** Fairly good and even, though inappropriately slow or rushed in places.
   - **C** A good, appropriate pace throughout.

Year 1/Primary 2, Summer 2: Fluency Check

Child's name: ________________ **Date:** ________

Fill in the table below. Consider whether any areas require targeted support for this child, or if your whole class would benefit from additional rehearsal or attention to a particular area.

Area of Focus	**Comments (include the appropriate A, B or C grading)**	**Requires targeted support?**
Decoding and Blending		
Expression		
Smoothness		
Punctuation		
Pace		

Guidance when deciding on next steps:

Decoding and Blending – ensure that the child reads a wider range of texts matched to their secure and current phonic knowledge to allow for application of their understanding. These should offer a wide range of vocabulary and language to ensure that children are developing their orthographic map. Children can re-read texts from earlier in the programme as well as read multiple texts from the same week to widen their application of their GPC knowledge.

For this assessment, further practice of these GPCs can be found in Essential Phonic Readers from Year One Summer 1:

Expression – use the weekly fluency texts and texts matched to the week of teaching to model reading with expression and intonation. Where appropriate, use echo or choral reading techniques to develop understanding of *how* to read a text with prosody.

Smoothness – additional practice of re-reading texts that use secure code knowledge. When assigning texts for home reading matched to current phonic knowledge for rehearsal, include a 'fluency' text that contain secure code knowledge. We recommend that children take home a book that is six weeks behind their 'current' knowledge book.

Punctuation – ensure that punctuation is explained and its impact on reading is modelled.

Pace – this should be modelled during all teacher-led reading. Re-reading texts will allow children to develop their reading 'at pace' as they become familiar with the text and its content.

There are many factors that can affect a child's reading on any one day. If a child's Fluency Check results don't reflect your knowledge of the child, consider running the check again using the alternative extract or a book at the same level, and use your own judgement when deciding which next steps to follow. The Fluency Check gives you a means of gaining additional information about a child's reading which you can use alongside everything else you know.

If children are not recognising the GPCs that they know in the text, they may require additional support with Blending for Reading. For this, you can use the ELS intervention.

The recycling plant turns old things into new things!

Engineers use special apparatus to break down objects. Then the objects can be reused. The engineers apply pressure. This squidges the items. Then they are turned into new things!

We can reuse paper, glass, plastic and metal. Recycling is good for the environment. It is good for the Earth's atmosphere, too.

We harm the Earth by cutting down trees. When we recycle, we reduce the harm we do.

Recycled glass can be used to make bottles and jars. Did you know that it can be used to make pipes and even road surfaces?

Year Two/P3 Autumn 1: Fluency Check

How do I complete this Fluency Check?

Before you start:

- Ensure that each child knows all the GPCs and HRSWs for Year One/P2 Summer 2. This is the content being reviewed in this fluency text.
- Children should have completed the ELS programme of study for Reception/P1 and Year One/P2. This assessment should take place in the half term *after* they have completed the ELS phonics programme. i.e. if a child completed ELS in the Summer Term of Year 1 they can move onto these progress checks. If they have completed ELS in the Autumn Term of Year 2/P3, then they should wait until Autumn 2 before beginning these fluency checks.
- Photocopy the assessment chart (page 61) so that you have a copy to fill in for each child.

Begin the Fluency Check:

- Ask the child to read the text for the first time without any pressure as a practice. This can be out loud or in their head. This particular text about penguins can be read more than once before the read given as the marker of progress. This is due to the high number of low-utility proper nouns which are key to the text but may be unfamiliar.
- For the second read, ask the children to read the text to you as 'smoothly' as possible. They are allowed to decode and blend if needed. If they do not know a HRSW, this can be given.
- If you feel that it would benefit to hear the text for a third time, please allow the child to read the text again.
- If the child requires support with a word, give it.
- Answer the questions as the child reads and straight after they have finished reading.

After the child has finished reading:

- Look at the guidance for next steps and determine how, if any, support should be directed.
- Consider how well you think the child understood what they were reading – considering the areas of focus. The questions to ask after the second reading of the text are there to interrogate each child's understanding of what they have read. Either through answering the question from memory or quickly locating the answer within the text. This can help you to track their progress towards the end of Key Stage 1 curriculum expectations.
- How did the child's voice sound as they read? Was it stilted or did they read it with expression and intonation that is appropriate for the text?

Year Two/P3 Autumn 1: Fluency Progress Check (teacher's copy)

Bold words contain GPCs taught in the second half of the Summer Term in Y1/P2.
Underlined words are HRSWs taught throughout the ELS Progression.

There was an exhibition at the **science** museum. It was about **penguins**. I learned a lot!

Penguins live near the sea and coasts. This is because they rely on the sea to find food. They can spend months at sea. **Penguins** are very good swimmers. They sometimes dive hundreds of **metres** deep in the sea. This is so they can find **enough** food. **Penguins** spend a lot of time in water. They come ashore to lay their eggs, **though**.

The **Macaroni penguin** is the most common **penguin**. It lives in places such as South America and Antarctica. These are cooler habitats.

Some breeds of **penguin** live in **warmer** places. One of these is the Galapagos **penguin**. These **penguins** live off the coast of **Ecuador**. This is a very rare breed of **penguin**.

Questions to ask when the child has read the text:

- Do all penguins live in cold habitats?
- Which are the most common penguins in the world?
- Where do the rarest penguins live?
- Was there anything that surprised you? If so, what and why?

The child can refer to the text if required.

Answer the following questions as the child reads and straight after they have finished reading:

1. **Decoding and Blending** Did the child need to decode and blend?
   - **A** Yes, many words were sounded out before blending.
   - **B** Unknown words were decoded and blended successfully.
   - **C** Very few, if any, words were decoded aloud.

Keep track of how many words are decoded and blended on the second (or third) read.

2. **Expression** Did the child attempt to speak with prosody and expression that indicated a good understanding of the text, e.g. to convey the mood or a character speaking?
   - **A** No, their expression and intonation did not indicate that they understood the text.
   - **B** Yes, they made some attempts to speak with expression and varied intonation.
   - **C** Yes, they spoke with lively and varied expression and intonation.

Did it sound as if the child spoke with an appropriate pattern of expression and intonation according to the content of the text? Did they demonstrate that they understood the text through their use of prosody?

3. **Smoothness** How smoothly did the child read the text?
   - **A** Not at all smoothly – reading was stilted and faltering throughout.
   - **B** Fairly smoothly – reading was mostly smooth but occasionally faltering.
   - **C** Very smooth – reading was smooth throughout.

Have they made progress after their initial reading of the text? Does it feel familiar or are they still decoding the same words as their initial reading?

4. **Punctuation and Phrasing** Did the child take notice of punctuation, for example pausing and phrasing the sentences appropriately?
   - **A** No, the child did not take any notice of punctuation.
   - **B** Yes, the child read and took notice of most punctuation.
   - **C** Yes, the child took notice of all punctuation.

Was their pausing appropriate?

5. **Pace** How was the child's pace of reading? Did the pace feel appropriate to the text? We do not recommend that you time the child – remember that pace can be too fast (indicating lack of comprehension) as well as too slow. Instead use your overall impression and judgement as to whether the pace felt right.
   - **A** Either too slow (signalling a lack of automaticity) or too rushed (signalling a lack of comprehension).
   - **B** Fairly good and even, though inappropriately slow or rushed in places.
   - **C** A good, appropriate pace throughout.

Did it sound natural as the child read the text?

Year 2/Primary 3, Autumn 1: Fluency Check

Child's name: ______________________ **Date:** ____________

Fill in the table below. Use A, B or C to determine specific support that may be required.

A – requires lots of support

B – requires some support

C – requires little to no support

Area of Focus		Consider appropriate support – see page 62.			Comments
		A	B	C	
1	Decoding and Blending				*How many words were overtly sounded and blended after a practice read?*
2	Expression				
3	Smoothness				
4	Punctuation				
5	Pace				

Guidance when deciding on next steps:

Decoding and Blending – ensure that children have adequate rehearsal of code that is secure along with re-reading of texts that have already been accessed. Children can take home additional decodable texts. If you believe that children require further practice for decoding and blending the GPCs within this assessment, the texts from Essential Phonic Readers Year 1 Summer 2 that can be sent home to further support are:

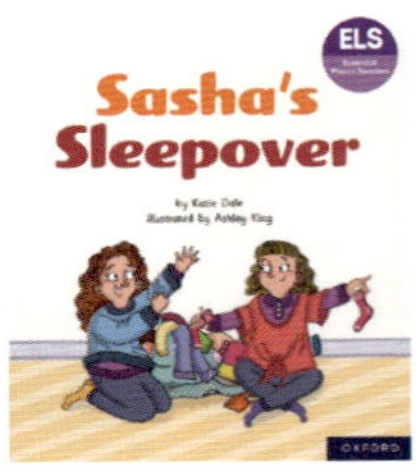

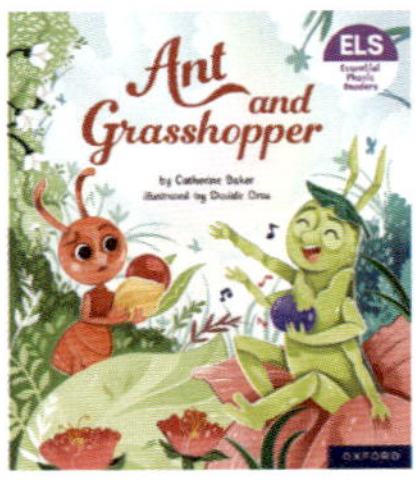

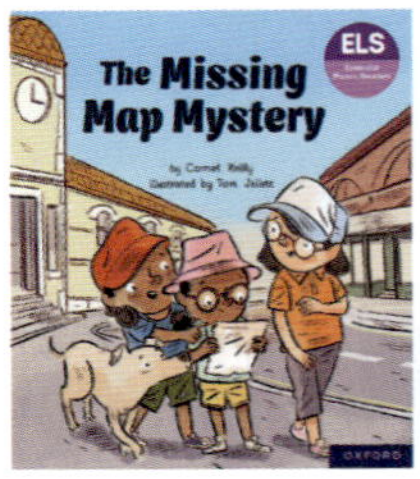

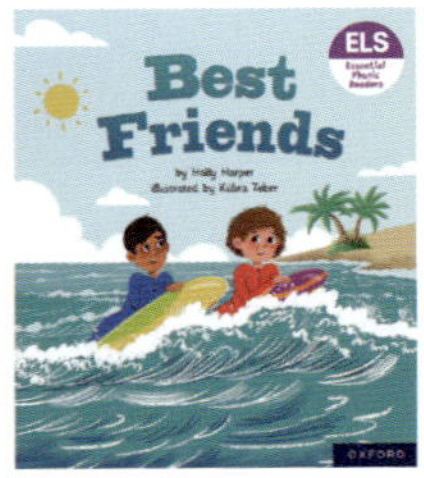

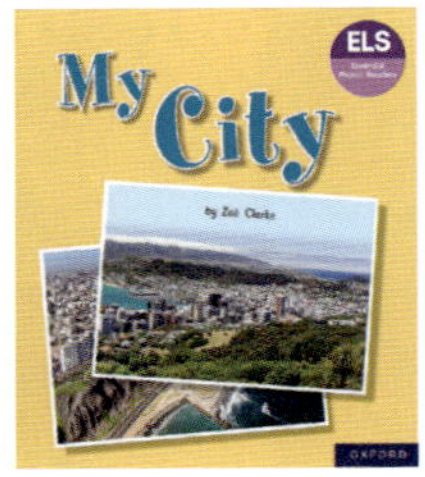

Expression – where appropriate, use 1:1 reading sessions to model and read parts of the text to and with the child. These sessions should take place in addition to group choral or echo reading. All adult reading, whether during lessons or during a protected 'story time' should demonstrate prosody.

Smoothness – additional practice of re-reading texts that use secure code knowledge. Ensure that children re-read texts that contain familiar code. This could mean that they re-read the same texts that were first given to match their current phonic knowledge.

Punctuation and Phrasing – ensure that punctuation and phrasing is explained and its impact on reading is modelled.

Pace – this should be modelled during all teacher-led reading. Re-reading texts will allow children to develop their reading 'at pace' as they become familiar with the text and its content.

There are many factors that can affect a child's reading on any one day. If a child's Fluency Check results don't reflect your knowledge of the child, consider running the check again using the alternative extract or a book at the same level, and use your own judgement when deciding which next steps to follow. The Fluency Check gives you a means of gaining additional information about a child's reading which you can use alongside everything else you know.

If children are not recognising the GPCs that they know in the text, they may require additional support with Blending for Reading. For this, you can use the ELS intervention.

If you recognise that there is a lack of 'fluency' when a child is reading, put in place support that will allow them to develop their reading fluency.

There was an exhibition at the science museum. It was about penguins. I learned a lot!

Penguins live near the sea and coasts. This is because they rely on the sea to find food. They can spend months at sea. Penguins are very good swimmers. They sometimes dive hundreds of metres deep in the sea. This is so they can find enough food. Penguins spend a lot of time in water. They come ashore to lay their eggs, though.

The Macaroni penguin is the most common penguin. It lives in places such as South America and Antarctica. These are cooler habitats.

Some breeds of penguin live in warmer places. One of these is the Galapagos penguin. These penguins live off the coast of Ecuador. This is a very rare breed of penguin.

Year Two/P3 Autumn 2: Fluency Check

How do I complete this Fluency Check?

Before you start:

- Ensure that each child have has completed the Autumn 1 content from ELS Essential Spelling. This content will be reviewed as part of this fluency text.
- Children should have completed the ELS programme of study for Reception/P1 and Year One/P2. This assessment should take place in the half term *after* they have completed the ELS phonics programme. i.e. if a child completed ELS in the Summer Term of Year 1 they can move onto these progress checks. If they have completed ELS in the Autumn Term of Year 2/P3, then they should wait until Autumn 2 before beginning these fluency checks.
- Photocopy the assessment chart (page 67) so that you have a copy to fill in for each child.

Begin the Fluency Check:

- Ask the child to read the text for the first time without any pressure as a practice. This can be out loud of in their head.
- For the second read, ask the children to read the text to you as 'smoothly' as possible. They are allowed to decode and blend if needed. If they do not know a HRSW, this can be given.
- If you feel that it would benefit to hear the text for a third time, please allow the child to read the text again.
- If the child requires support with a word, give it.
- Answer the questions as the child reads and straight after they have finished reading.

After the child has finished reading:

- Look at the guidance for next steps and determine how, if any, support should be directed.
- Consider how well you think the child understood what they were reading – considering the areas of focus. The questions to ask after the second reading of the text are there to interrogate each child's understanding of what they have read. Either through answering the question from memory or quickly locating the answer within the text. This can help you to track their progress towards the end of Key Stage 1 curriculum expectations.
- How did the child's voice sound as they read? Was it stilted or did they read it with expression and intonation that is appropriate for the text.

Year Two/P3 Autumn 2: Fluency Progress Check (teacher's copy)

Bold words contain focus spellings taught in the first half of the Autumn Term in Y2/P2.
Underlined words are HRSWs taught throughout the ELS Progression.

We **drove** across the **valley** to my **hockey** competition. I was a bit **worried** because I had a sore **wrist**. I **might** not be allowed to **play**.

Concerned, my **coach walked over** to me.

"If you **feel** well enough to **play**, wear **these**," she said.

She **gave** me a **wrist** guard and glove. The **wrist** guard would **protect** my **wrist**. The glove would **protect** my hand. I felt so much better!

"I'm **excited** to **play** now," I said to my friend. She was a **pupil** at school with me.

As we **waited** to start, I had a **slice** of melon. **Soon**, it was our turn to **play**. The **whole team charged** onto the **centre** of the pitch.

"Go **team**!" the **whole team** shouted.

I **knew** we were going to **play** a **great game**!

Questions to ask when the child has read the text:

- Why was the player worried?
- What two things did the coach give them?
- How did these items make the player feel?
- At the end, was the player looking forward to the game? How do you know?

The child can refer to the text if required.

Answer the following questions as the child reads and straight after they have finished reading:

1. **Decoding and Blending** Did the child need to decode and blend?
   - **A** Yes, many words were sounded out before blending.
   - **B** Unknown words were decoded and blended successfully.
   - **C** Very few, if any, words were decoded aloud.

Keep track of how many words are decoded and blended on the second (or third) read.

2. **Expression** Did the child attempt to speak with prosody and expression that indicated a good understanding of the text, e.g. to convey the mood or a character speaking?
   - **A** No, their expression and intonation did not indicate that they understood the text.
   - **B** Yes, they made some attempts to speak with expression and varied intonation.
   - **C** Yes, they spoke with lively and varied expression and intonation.

Did it sound as if the child spoke with an appropriate pattern of expression and intonation according to the content of the text? Did they demonstrate that they understood the text through their use of prosody?

3. **Smoothness** How smoothly did the child read the text?
   - **A** Not at all smoothly – reading was stilted and faltering throughout.
   - **B** Fairly smoothly – reading was mostly smooth but occasionally faltering.
   - **C** Very smooth – reading was smooth throughout.

Have they made progress after their initial reading of the text? Does it feel familiar or are they still decoding the same words as their initial reading?

4. **Punctuation and Phrasing** Did the child take notice of punctuation, for example pausing and phrasing the sentences appropriately?
   - **A** No, the child did not take any notice of punctuation.
   - **B** Yes, the child read and took notice of most punctuation.
   - **C** Yes, the child took notice of all punctuation.

Was their pausing appropriate?

5. **Pace** How was the child's pace of reading? Did the pace feel appropriate to the text? We do not recommend that you time the child – remember that pace can be too fast (indicating lack of comprehension) as well as too slow. Instead use your overall impression and judgement as to whether the pace felt right.
   - **A** Either too slow (signalling a lack of automaticity) or too rushed (signalling a lack of comprehension).
   - **B** Fairly good and even, though inappropriately slow or rushed in places.
   - **C** A good, appropriate pace throughout.

Did it sound natural as the child read the text?

Year 2/Primary 3, Autumn 2: Fluency Check

Child's name: | **Date:**

Fill in the table below. Use A, B or C to determine specific support that may be required.

A – requires lots of support

B – requires some support

C – requires little to no support

Area of Focus		Consider appropriate support – see page 68.			Comments
		A	B	C	
1	Decoding and Blending				*How many words were overtly sounded and blended after a practice read?*
2	Expression				
3	Smoothness				
4	Punctuation				
5	Pace				

Guidance when deciding on next steps:

Decoding and Blending – ensure that children have adequate rehearsal of code that is secure along with re-reading of texts that have already been accessed. Children can take home additional decodable texts. If you believe that children require further practice for decoding and blending the GPCs within this assessment, the texts from Essential Phonic Readers Year 1 Summer 2 that can be sent home to further support are:

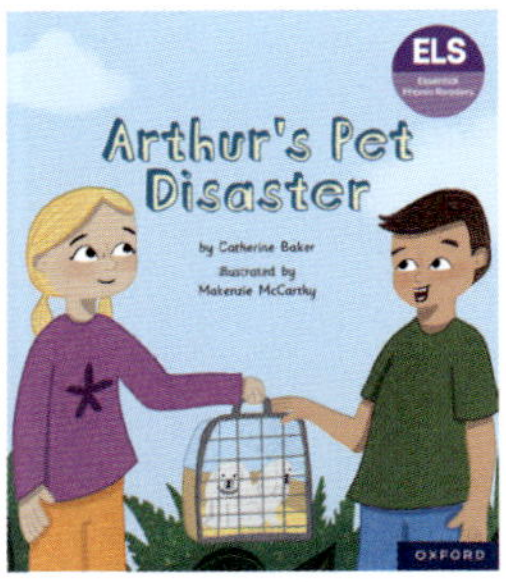

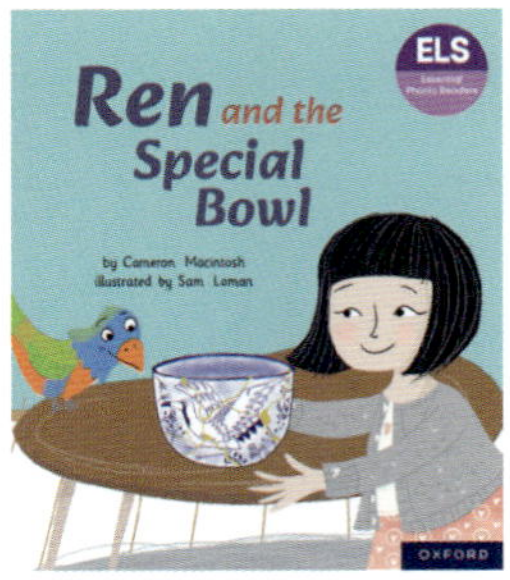

Expression – where appropriate, use 1:1 reading sessions to model and read parts of the text to and with the child. These sessions should take place in addition to group choral or echo reading. All adult reading, whether during lessons or during a protected 'story time' should demonstrate prosody.

Smoothness – additional practice of re-reading texts that use secure code knowledge. Ensure that children re-read texts that contain familiar code. This could mean that they re-read the same texts that were first given to match their current phonic knowledge.

Punctuation and Phrasing – ensure that punctuation and phrasing is explained and its impact on reading is modelled.

Pace – this should be modelled during all teacher-led reading. Re-reading texts will allow children to develop their reading 'at pace' as they become familiar with the text and its content.

There are many factors that can affect a child's reading on any one day. If a child's Fluency Check results don't reflect your knowledge of the child, consider running the check again using the alternative extract or a book at the same level, and use your own judgement when deciding which next steps to follow. The Fluency Check gives you a means of gaining additional information about a child's reading which you can use alongside everything else you know.

If children are not recognising the GPCs that they know in the text, they may require additional support with Blending for Reading. For this, you can use the ELS intervention.

If you recognise that there is a lack of 'fluency' when a child is reading, put in place support that will allow them to develop their reading fluency.

We drove across the valley to my hockey competition. I was a bit worried because I had a sore wrist. I might not be allowed to play.

Concerned, my coach walked over to me.

"If you feel well enough to play, wear these," she said.

She gave me a wrist guard and glove. The wrist guard would protect my wrist. The glove would protect my hand. I felt so much better!

"I'm excited to play now," I said to my friend. She was a pupil at school with me.

As we waited to start, I had a slice of melon. Soon, it was our turn to play. The whole team charged onto the centre of the pitch.

"Go team!" the whole team shouted.

I knew we were going to play a great game!

Year Two/P3 Spring 1: Fluency Check

How do I complete this Fluency Check?

Before you start:

- Ensure that each child has completed the Autumn 2 content from ELS Essential Spelling. This content will be reviewed as part of this fluency text.
- Children should have completed the ELS programme of study for Reception/P1 and Year 1/P2. This assessment should take place in the half term *after* they have completed the ELS phonics programme. i.e. if a child completed ELS in the Summer Term of Year 1 they can move onto these progress checks. If they have completed ELS in the Autumn Term of Year 2/P3, then they should wait until Autumn 2 before beginning these fluency checks.
- Photocopy the assessment chart (page 73) so that you have a copy to fill in for each child.

Begin the Fluency Check:

- Ask the child to read the text for the first time without any pressure as a practice. This can be out loud or in their head.
- For the second read, ask the children to read the text to you as 'smoothly' as possible. They are allowed to decode and blend if needed. If they do not know a HRSW, this can be given.
- If you feel that it would benefit to hear the text for a third time, please allow the child to read the text again.
- If the child requires support with a word, give it.
- Answer the questions as the child reads and straight after they have finished reading.

After the child has finished reading:

- Look at the guidance for next steps and determine how, if any, support should be directed.
- Consider how well you think the child understood what they were reading – considering the areas of focus. The questions to ask after the second reading of the text are there to interrogate each child's understanding of what they have read. Either through answering the question from memory or quickly locating the answer within the text. This can help you to track their progress towards the end of Key Stage 1 curriculum expectations.
- How did the child's voice sound as they read? Was it stilted or did they read it with expression and intonation that is appropriate for the text?

Year Two/P3 Spring 1: Fluency Progress Check (teacher's copy)

Bold words contain focus spellings taught in the second half of the Autumn Term in Y2/P2.
Underlined words are HRSWs taught throughout the ELS Progression.

Our neighbours **moved recently. Removal** vans can **usually** park in the car park. Today, the car park was too crowded. The truck had to pull up outside our block of flats.

I watched as the truck rolled up. The name of the **company** was '**Knights Movers**'. They had a **sign** on the side. It was a chess set and a **knight**.

"What do you think the **sign** means?" I asked Mum.

"I think it means they **move** your things like you **move** the **pieces** on a chess board," Mum replied.

I saw the **removal** people going in and out all day. They **worked** in pairs. They **worked** quickly. They carried out heavy things on a **trolley**. Two boxes had **writing** on them.

"That is so the **removal** people **know** where to put them in the new **place**," Mum said.

Finally, they carried out a **huge fridge** and a **television**. The **whole** house was empty.

Questions to ask when the child has read the text:

- Why did the truck have to park outside the block of flats?
- What was the moving company called?
- Why did the child's mum think that was their name?
- Can you name one thing they carried out of the flat?

The child can refer to the text if required.

Answer the following questions as the child reads and straight after they have finished reading:

1. **Decoding and Blending** Did the child need to decode and blend?

   A Yes, many words were sounded out before blending.

   B Unknown words were decoded and blended successfully.

   C Very few, if any, words were decoded aloud.

Keep track of how many words are decoded and blended on the second (or third) read.

2. **Expression** Did the child attempt to speak with prosody and expression that indicated a good understanding of the text, e.g. to convey the mood or a character speaking?

   A No, their expression and intonation did not indicate that they understood the text.

   B Yes, they made some attempts to speak with expression and varied intonation.

   C Yes, they spoke with lively and varied expression and intonation.

Did it sound as if the child spoke with an appropriate pattern of expression and intonation according to the content of the text? Did they demonstrate that they understood the text through their use of prosody?

3. **Smoothness** How smoothly did the child read the text?

   A Not at all smoothly – reading was stilted and faltering throughout.

   B Fairly smoothly – reading was mostly smooth but occasionally faltering.

   C Very smooth – reading was smooth throughout.

Have they made progress after their initial reading of the text? Does it feel familiar or are they still decoding the same words as their initial reading?

4. **Punctuation and Phrasing** Did the child take notice of punctuation, for example pausing and phrasing the sentences appropriately?

   A No, the child did not take any notice of punctuation.

   B Yes, the child read and took notice of most punctuation.

   C Yes, the child took notice of all punctuation.

Was their pausing appropriate?

5. **Pace** How was the child's pace of reading? Did the pace feel appropriate to the text? We do not recommend that you time the child – remember that pace can be too fast (indicating lack of comprehension) as well as too slow. Instead use your overall impression and judgement as to whether the pace felt right.

   A Either too slow (signalling a lack of automaticity) or too rushed (signalling a lack of comprehension).

   B Fairly good and even, though inappropriately slow or rushed in places.

   C A good, appropriate pace throughout.

Did it sound natural as the child read the text?

Year 2/Primary 3, Spring 1: Fluency Check

Child's name: **Date:**

Fill in the table below. Use A, B or C to determine specific support that may be required.

A – requires lots of support

B – requires some support

C – requires little to no support

Area of Focus		Consider appropriate support – see page 74.			Comments
		A	B	C	
1	Decoding and Blending				*How many words were overtly sounded and blended after a practice read?*
2	Expression				
3	Smoothness				
4	Punctuation				
5	Pace				

Guidance when deciding on next steps:

Decoding and Blending – ensure that children have adequate rehearsal of code that is secure along with re-reading of texts that have already been accessed. Where children require further support with reading longer words, this can be achieved through repeated rehearsal using the texts from *Fluency Anthology 2* for this half term and the readers listed below.

For this assessment, further practice of these GPCs can be found in Readerful Level 8:

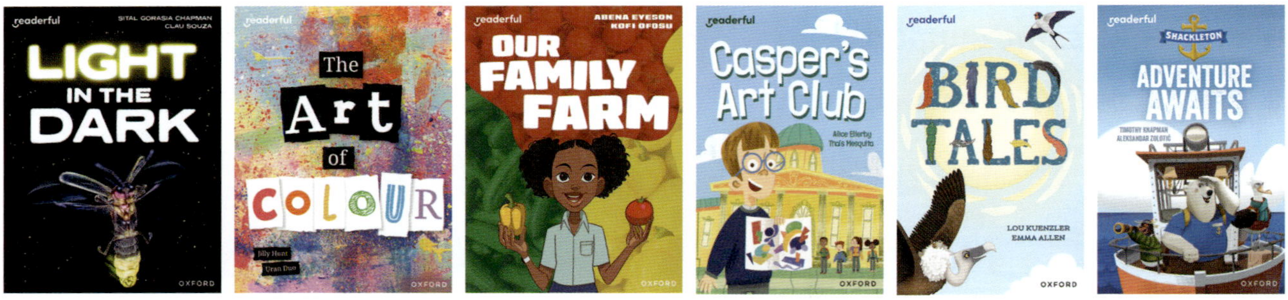

Expression – where appropriate, use 1:1 reading sessions to model and read parts of the text to and with the child. These sessions should take place in addition to group choral or echo reading. All adult reading, whether during lessons or during a protected 'story time' should demonstrate prosody.

Smoothness – additional practice of re-reading texts that use secure code knowledge. Ensure that children re-read texts that contain familiar code. This could mean that they re-read the same texts that were first given to match their current phonic knowledge.

Punctuation and Phrasing – ensure that punctuation and phrasing is explained and its impact on reading is modelled.

Pace – this should be modelled during all teacher-led reading. Re-reading texts will allow children to develop their reading 'at pace' as they become familiar with the text and its content.

There are many factors that can affect a child's reading on any one day. If a child's Fluency Check results don't reflect your knowledge of the child, consider running the check again using the alternative extract or a book at the same level, and use your own judgement when deciding which next steps to follow. The Fluency Check gives you a means of gaining additional information about a child's reading which you can use alongside everything else you know.

If children are not recognising the GPCs that they know in the text, they may require additional support with Blending for Reading. For this, you can use the ELS intervention.

If you recognise that there is a lack of 'fluency' when a child is reading, put in place support that will allow them to develop their reading fluency.

Our neighbours moved recently. Removal vans can usually park in the car park. Today, the car park was too crowded. The truck had to pull up outside our block of flats.

I watched as the truck rolled up. The name of the company was 'Knights Movers'. They had a sign on the side. It was a chess set and a knight.

"What do you think the sign means?" I asked Mum.

"I think it means they move your things like you move the pieces on a chess board," Mum replied.

I saw the removal people going in and out all day. They worked in pairs. They worked quickly. They carried out heavy things on a trolley. Two boxes had writing on them.

"That is so the removal people know where to put them in the new place," Mum said.

Finally, they carried out a huge fridge and a television. The whole house was empty.

Year Two/P3 Spring 2: Fluency Check

How do I complete this Fluency Check?

Before you start:

- Ensure that each child has completed the Spring 1 content from ELS Essential Spelling. This content will be reviewed as part of this fluency text.
- Children should have completed the ELS programme of study for Reception/P1 and Year One/P2. This assessment should take place in the half term *after* they have completed the ELS phonics programme. i.e. if a child completed ELS in the Summer Term of Year 1 they can move onto these progress checks. If they have completed ELS in the Autumn Term of Year 2/P3, then they should wait until Autumn 2 before beginning these fluency checks.
- Photocopy the assessment chart (page 79) so that you have a copy to fill in for each child.

Begin the Fluency Check:

- Ask the child to read the text for the first time without any pressure as a practice. This can be out loud or in their head.
- For the second read, ask the children to read the text to you as 'smoothly' as possible. They are allowed to decode and blend if needed. If they do not know a HRSW, this can be given.
- If you feel that it would benefit to hear the text for a third time, please allow the child to read the text again.
- If the child requires support with a word, give it.
- Answer the questions as the child reads and straight after they have finished reading.

After the child has finished reading:

- Look at the guidance for next steps and determine how, if any, support should be directed.
- Consider how well you think the child understood what they were reading – considering the areas of focus. The questions to ask after the second reading of the text are there to interrogate each child's understanding of what they have read. Either through answering the question from memory or quickly locating the answer within the text. This can help you to track their progress towards the end of Key Stage 1 curriculum expectations.
- How did the child's voice sound as they read? Was it stilted or did they read it with expression and intonation that is appropriate for the text?

Bold words contain focus spellings taught in the first half of the Spring Term in Y2/P2.
Underlined words are HRSWs taught throughout the ELS Progression.

We can study **artefacts** from history to find out about how people lived. These are some common items from the Tudor times (1485–1603). I wonder if we still use or see any of these today.

Purses

These were worn on the outside of garments. They were filled with **chopped** herbs and **petals**. The contents of the bag were intended to mask any bad smells! These bags had delicate stitching on them. We think that people **planned** for them to be seen.

Toasting forks

These were used to cook snacks. Tudor people would toast **apples** or pears. These toasting forks were long to get the snack to the **hottest** part of the fire without burning their fingers! The fork was often made of **metal**, but the **handle** was not. This meant that whilst the fork got **hotter**, the **handle** did **not**.

Jugs

Jugs were used to store and serve liquids. In Tudor times, the range of colours was quite limited. However, a green colour on the outside of the jug could be **made**. This was done by adding little bits of copper when the jug was put in the fire to harden.

Questions to ask when the child has read the text:

- Why did people wear a purse?
- Do we use anything to mask smells?
- Have you ever seen a toasting fork?
- How did they make green jugs in Tudor times?

The child can refer to the text if required.

Answer the following questions as the child reads and straight after they have finished reading:

1. **Decoding and Blending** Did the child need to decode and blend?
   - **A** Yes, many words were sounded out before blending.
   - **B** Unknown words were decoded and blended successfully.
   - **C** Very few, if any, words were decoded aloud.

Keep track of how many words are decoded and blended on the second (or third) read.

2. **Expression** Did the child attempt to speak with prosody and expression that indicated a good understanding of the text, e.g. to convey the mood or a character speaking?
   - **A** No, their expression and intonation did not indicate that they understood the text.
   - **B** Yes, they made some attempts to speak with expression and varied intonation.
   - **C** Yes, they spoke with lively and varied expression and intonation.

Did it sound as if the child spoke with an appropriate pattern of expression and intonation according to the content of the text? Did they demonstrate that they understood the text through their use of prosody?

3. **Smoothness** How smoothly did the child read the text?
   - **A** Not at all smoothly – reading was stilted and faltering throughout.
   - **B** Fairly smoothly – reading was mostly smooth but occasionally faltering.
   - **C** Very smooth – reading was smooth throughout.

Have they made progress after their initial reading of the text? Does it feel familiar or are they still decoding the same words as their initial reading?

4. **Punctuation and Phrasing** Did the child take notice of punctuation, for example pausing and phrasing the sentences appropriately?
   - **A** No, the child did not take any notice of punctuation.
   - **B** Yes, the child read and took notice of most punctuation.
   - **C** Yes, the child took notice of all punctuation.

Was their pausing appropriate?

5. **Pace** How was the child's pace of reading? Did the pace feel appropriate to the text? We do not recommend that you time the child – remember that pace can be too fast (indicating lack of comprehension) as well as too slow. Instead use your overall impression and judgement as to whether the pace felt right.
   - **A** Either too slow (signalling a lack of automaticity) or too rushed (signalling a lack of comprehension).
   - **B** Fairly good and even, though inappropriately slow or rushed in places.
   - **C** A good, appropriate pace throughout.

Did it sound natural as the child read the text?

Year 2/Primary 3, Spring 2: Fluency Check

Child's name: ______________ **Date:** ______________

Fill in the table below. Use A, B or C to determine specific support that may be required.

A – requires lots of support

B – requires some support

C – requires little to no support

Area of Focus		Consider appropriate support – see page 80.			Comments
		A	**B**	**C**	
1	Decoding and Blending				*How many words were overtly sounded and blended after a practice read?*
2	Expression				
3	Smoothness				
4	Punctuation				
5	Pace				

Guidance when deciding on next steps:

Decoding and Blending – ensure that children have adequate rehearsal of code that is secure along with re-reading of texts that have already been accessed. Where children require further support with reading longer words, this can be achieved through repeated rehearsal using the texts from *Fluency Anthology 2* for this half term and the readers listed below.

For this assessment, further practice of these GPCs can be found in Readerful Level 9:

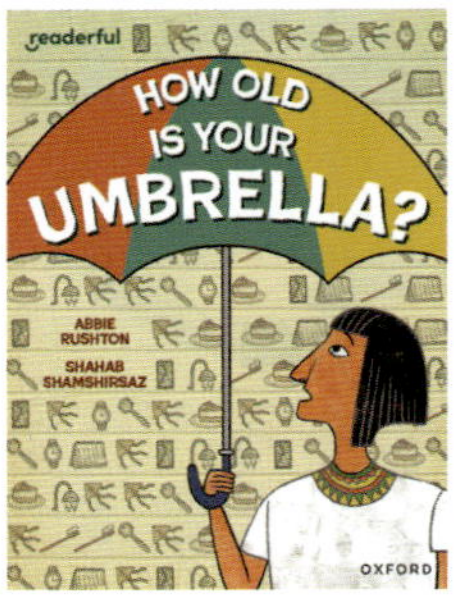

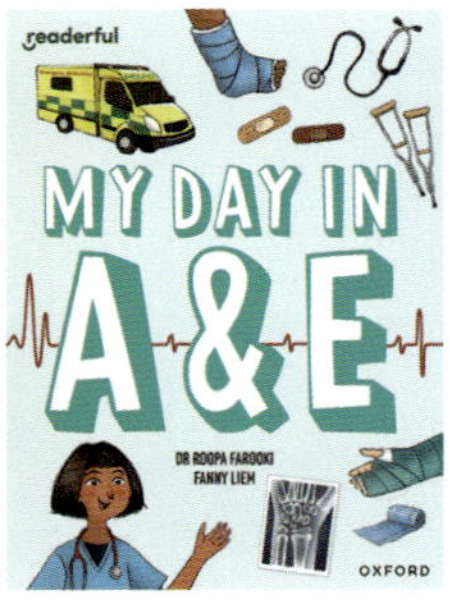

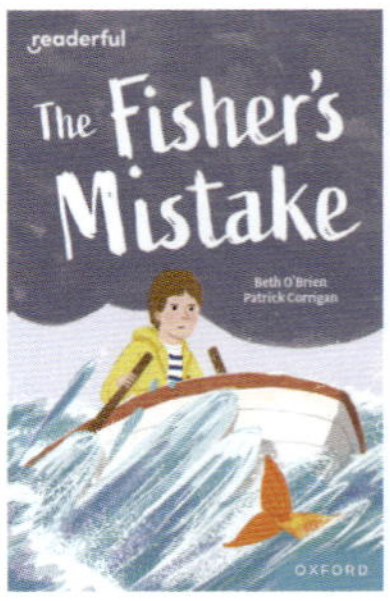

Expression – where appropriate, use 1:1 reading sessions to model and read parts of the text to and with the child. These sessions should take place in addition to group choral or echo reading. All adult reading, whether during lessons or during a protected 'story time' should demonstrate prosody.

Smoothness – additional practice of re-reading texts that use secure code knowledge. Ensure that children re-read texts that contain familiar code. This could mean that they re-read the same texts that were first given to match their current phonic knowledge.

Punctuation and Phrasing – ensure that punctuation and phrasing is explained and its impact on reading is modelled.

Pace – this should be modelled during all teacher-led reading. Re-reading texts will allow children to develop their reading 'at pace' as they become familiar with the text and its content.

There are many factors that can affect a child's reading on any one day. If a child's Fluency Check results don't reflect your knowledge of the child, consider running the check again using the alternative extract or a book at the same level, and use your own judgement when deciding which next steps to follow. The Fluency Check gives you a means of gaining additional information about a child's reading which you can use alongside everything else you know.

If children are not recognising the GPCs that they know in the text, they may require additional support with Blending for Reading. For this, you can use the ELS intervention.

If you recognise that there is a lack of 'fluency' when a child is reading, put in place support that will allow them to develop their reading fluency.

We can study artefacts from history to find out about how people lived.

These are some common items from the Tudor times (1485–1603). I wonder if we still use or see any of these today.

Purses

These were worn on the outside of garments. They were filled with chopped herbs and petals. The contents of the bag were intended to mask any bad smells! These bags had delicate stitching on them. We think that people planned for them to be seen.

Toasting forks

These were used to cook snacks. Tudor people would toast apples or pears. These toasting forks were long so people could get the snack to the hottest part of the fire without burning their fingers! The fork was often made of metal, but the handle was not. This meant that whilst the fork got hotter, the handle did not.

Jugs

Jugs were used to store and serve liquids. In Tudor times, the range of colours was quite limited. However, a green colour on the outside of the jug could be made. This was done by adding little bits of copper when the jug was put in the fire to harden.

Year Two/P3 Summer 1: Fluency Check

How do I complete this Fluency Check?

Before you start:

- Ensure that each child has completed the Spring 1 content ELS Essential Spelling.
- Children should have completed the ELS programme of study for Reception/P1 and Year One/P2. This assessment should take place in the half term *after* they have completed the ELS phonics programme. i.e. if a child completed ELS in the Summer Term of Year 1 they can move onto these progress checks. If they have completed ELS in the Autumn Term of Year 2/P3, then they should wait until Autumn 2 before beginning these fluency checks.
- Photocopy the assessment chart (page 85) so that you have a copy to fill in for each child.

Begin the Fluency Check:

- Ask the child to read the text for the first time without any pressure as a practice. This can be out loud or in their head.
- For the second read, ask the children to read the text to you as 'smoothly' as possible. They are allowed to decode and blend if needed. If they do not know a HRSW, this can be given.
- If you feel that it would benefit to hear the text for a third time, please allow the child to read the text again.
- If the child requires support with a word, give it.
- Answer the questions as the child reads and straight after they have finished reading.

After the child has finished reading:

- Look at the guidance for next steps and determine how, if any, support should be directed.
- Consider how well you think the child understood what they were reading – considering the areas of focus. The questions to ask after the second reading of the text are there to interrogate each child's understanding of what they have read. Either through answering the question from memory or quickly locating the answer within the text. This can help you to track their progress towards the end of Key Stage 1 curriculum expectations.
- How did the child's voice sound as they read? Was it stilted or did they read it with expression and intonation that is appropriate for the text?

Bold words contain focus spellings taught in the second half of the Spring Term in Y2/P2. Underlined words are HRSWs taught throughout the ELS Progression.

Samuel stood at the side of the stage. It **wasn't** his turn to go out yet. He watched as the other **dancers** flew through the air in their **shiny**, **sparkly** costumes. He **smiled** to himself. He was so proud of the **dancers** on stage. They had all worked hard to make this show happen.

The **dancers** had funded the show by selling their time and skills. One group had **baked** cakes to sell. One pair had **served** teas at local parties. Others had done **filing** for a local company. They were not the **largest** dance company, but everyone had played a part.

Mo had a good idea. "**Rather** than **using** professional flyers, I will design them," he said to Samuel. This **saved** a lot of money. Everyone had helped to hand them out around the town.

Some of the **dancers** planned a mini show in the town square. This got a lot of **attention**.

Finally, it was time for the performance. It was Samuel's moment to shine. He **danced** onto the stage and looked out at the people watching. They **smiled** and clapped as he began his performance. He had never **smiled** so much in his life. He **couldn't** believe how many people were in the audience.

Questions to ask when the child has read the text:

- Why was Samuel proud?
- What were some of the ways that the dancers raised money?
- How did you know that the dancers in the town square were good?
- How do you think Samuel felt when he was on stage?

The child can refer to the text if required.

Answer the following questions as the child reads and straight after they have finished reading:

1. **Decoding and Blending** Did the child need to decode and blend?

   A Yes, many words were sounded out before blending.

   B Unknown words were decoded and blended successfully.

   C Very few, if any, words were decoded aloud.

Keep track of how many words are decoded and blended on the second (or third) read.

2. **Expression** Did the child attempt to speak with prosody and expression that indicated a good understanding of the text, e.g. to convey the mood or a character speaking?

   A No, their expression and intonation did not indicate that they understood the text.

   B Yes, they made some attempts to speak with expression and varied intonation.

   C Yes, they spoke with lively and varied expression and intonation.

Did it sound as if the child spoke with an appropriate pattern of expression and intonation according to the content of the text? Did they demonstrate that they understood the text through their use of prosody?

3. **Smoothness** How smoothly did the child read the text?

   A Not at all smoothly – reading was stilted and faltering throughout.

   B Fairly smoothly – reading was mostly smooth but occasionally faltering.

   C Very smooth – reading was smooth throughout.

Have they made progress after their initial reading of the text? Does it feel familiar or are they still decoding the same words as their initial reading?

4. **Punctuation and Phrasing** Did the child take notice of punctuation, for example pausing and phrasing the sentences appropriately?

   A No, the child did not take any notice of punctuation.

   B Yes, the child read and took notice of most punctuation.

   C Yes, the child took notice of all punctuation.

Was their pausing appropriate?

5. **Pace** How was the child's pace of reading? Did the pace feel appropriate to the text? We do not recommend that you time the child – remember that pace can be too fast (indicating lack of comprehension) as well as too slow. Instead use your overall impression and judgement as to whether the pace felt right.

   A Either too slow (signalling a lack of automaticity) or too rushed (signalling a lack of comprehension).

   B Fairly good and even, though inappropriately slow or rushed in places.

   C A good, appropriate pace throughout.

Did it sound natural as the child read the text?

Year 2/Primary 3, Summer 1: Fluency Check

Child's name: **Date:**

Fill in the table below. Use A, B or C to determine specific support that may be required.

A – requires lots of support

B – requires some support

C – requires little to no support

Area of Focus		Consider appropriate support – see page 86.			Comments
		A	B	C	
1	Decoding and Blending				*How many words were overtly sounded and blended after a practice read?*
2	Expression				
3	Smoothness				
4	Punctuation				
5	Pace				

Guidance when deciding on next steps:

Decoding and Blending – ensure that children have adequate rehearsal of code that is secure along with re-reading of texts that have already been accessed. Where children require further support with reading longer words, this can be achieved through repeated rehearsal using the texts from *Fluency Anthology 2* for this half term and the readers listed below.

For this assessment, further practice of these GPCs can be found in Readerful Level 10:

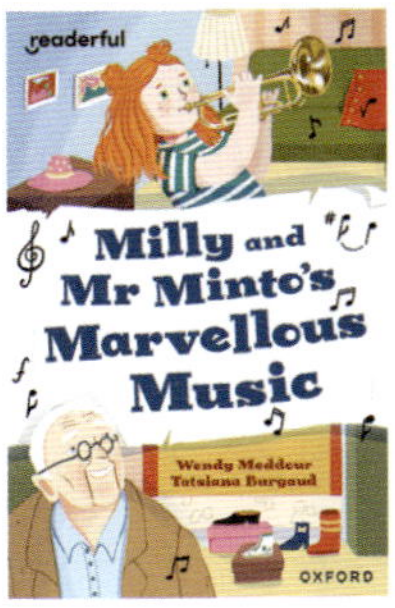

Expression – where appropriate, use 1:1 reading sessions to model and read parts of the text to and with the child. These sessions should take place in addition to group choral or echo reading. All adult reading, whether during lessons or during a protected 'story time' should demonstrate prosody.

Smoothness – additional practice of re-reading texts that use secure code knowledge. Ensure that children re-read texts that contain familiar code. This could mean that they re-read the same texts that were first given to match their current phonic knowledge.

Punctuation and Phrasing – ensure that punctuation and phrasing is explained and its impact on reading is modelled.

Pace – this should be modelled during all teacher-led reading. Re-reading texts will allow children to develop their reading 'at pace' as they become familiar with the text and its content.

There are many factors that can affect a child's reading on any one day. If a child's Fluency Check results don't reflect your knowledge of the child, consider running the check again using the alternative extract or a book at the same level, and use your own judgement when deciding which next steps to follow. The Fluency Check gives you a means of gaining additional information about a child's reading which you can use alongside everything else you know.

If children are not recognising the GPCs that they know in the text, they may require additional support with Blending for Reading. For this, you can use the ELS intervention.

If you recognise that there is a lack of 'fluency' when a child is reading, put in place support that will allow them to develop their reading fluency.

Samuel stood at the side of the stage. It wasn't his turn to go out yet. He watched as the other dancers flew through the air in their shiny, sparkly costumes. He smiled to himself. He was so proud of the dancers on stage. They had all worked hard to make this show happen.

The dancers had funded the show by selling their time and skills. One group had baked cakes to sell. One pair had served teas at local parties. Others had done filing for a local company. They were not the largest dance company, but everyone had played a part.

Mo had a good idea. "Rather than using professional flyers, I will design them," he said to Samuel. This saved a lot of money. Everyone had helped to hand them out around the town.

Some of the dancers planned a mini show in the town square. This got a lot of attention.

Finally, it was time for the performance. It was Samuel's moment to shine. He danced onto the stage and looked out at the people watching. They smiled and clapped as he began his performance. He had never smiled so much in his life. He couldn't believe how many people were in the audience.

Year Two/P3 Summer 2: Fluency Check

How do I complete this Fluency Check?

Before you start:

- If you are using Essential Spelling for Year 2, ensure that each child has completed the Spring 2 content of ELS Essential Spelling.
- Children should have completed the ELS programme of study for Reception/P1 and Year One/P2. This assessment should take place in the half term *after* they have completed the ELS phonics programme. i.e. if a child completed ELS in the Summer Term of Year 1 they can move onto these progress checks. If they have completed ELS in the Autumn Term of Year 2/P3, then they should wait until Autumn 2 before beginning these fluency checks.
- Photocopy the assessment chart (page 91) so that you have a copy to fill in for each child.

Begin the Fluency Check:

- Ask the child to read the text for the first time without any pressure as a practice. This can be out loud or in their head.
- For the second read, ask the children to read the text to you as 'smoothly' as possible. They are allowed to decode and blend if needed. If they do not know a HRSW, this can be given.
- If you feel that it would benefit to hear the text for a third time, please allow the child to read the text again.
- If the child requires support with a word, give it.
- Answer the questions as the child reads and straight after they have finished reading.

After the child has finished reading:

- Look at the guidance for next steps and determine how, if any, support should be directed.
- Consider how well you think the child understood what they were reading – considering the areas of focus. The questions to ask after the second reading of the text are there to interrogate each child's understanding of what they have read. Either through answering the question from memory or quickly locating the answer within the text. This can help you to track their progress towards the end of Key Stage 1 curriculum expectations.
- How did the child's voice sound as they read? Was it stilted or did they read it with expression and intonation that is appropriate for the text?

Bold words contain focus spellings taught in the first half of the Summer Term in Y2/P2.
Underlined words are HRSWs taught throughout the ELS Progression.

Our roads and public transport have to be properly maintained. This can mean that there are **replacement** services while the work is taking place.

The company making the repairs must work as **quickly** as possible. You might see **brightly** lit signs telling you what is happening. When workers are by the roadside, they must be **careful**. This means that some road works are done overnight when it is quieter.

The train **replacements** can sometimes cause **disappointment**. They can be much slower than the trains! However, if we don't have the tracks replaced or repaired, it could be dangerous.

When the roads and trains are **carefully** maintained and **improvements** are made, people often feel relieved. This is because their journeys will **hopefully** be less **stressful**. There will be fewer delays. This means their journeys are safer and quicker.

When you see a notice for a road **improvement** or a train **replacement**, remember this is to help us. **Countless** people will have better journeys.

Our public transport services help us to travel with ease. Often, they are better for the **environment**, too.

Have you ever been on public transport? Have you ever seen a road closed or a train **replacement** service?

Questions to ask when the child has read the text:

- Why do you think it can be frustrating if the train or road is closed?

The child can refer to the text if required.

Ask the child to answer the two questions within the text.

- Have you ever been on public transport?
- Have you ever seen a road closed or a train on rail replacement?

Answer the following questions as the child reads and straight after they have finished reading:

1. **Decoding and Blending** Did the child need to decode and blend?
   - **A** Yes, many words were sounded out before blending.
   - **B** Unknown words were decoded and blended successfully.
   - **C** Very few, if any, words were decoded aloud.

Keep track of how many words are decoded and blended on the second (or third) read.

2. **Expression** Did the child attempt to speak with prosody and expression that indicated a good understanding of the text, e.g. to convey the mood or a character speaking?
   - **A** No, their expression and intonation did not indicate that they understood the text.
   - **B** Yes, they made some attempts to speak with expression and varied intonation.
   - **C** Yes, they spoke with lively and varied expression and intonation.

Did it sound as if the child spoke with an appropriate pattern of expression and intonation according to the content of the text? Did they demonstrate that they understood the text through their use of prosody?

3. **Smoothness** How smoothly did the child read the text?
   - **A** Not at all smoothly – reading was stilted and faltering throughout.
   - **B** Fairly smoothly – reading was mostly smooth but occasionally faltering.
   - **C** Very smooth – reading was smooth throughout.

Have they made progress after their initial reading of the text? Does it feel familiar or are they still decoding the same words as their initial reading?

4. **Punctuation and Phrasing** Did the child take notice of punctuation, for example pausing and phrasing the sentences appropriately?
   - **A** No, the child did not take any notice of punctuation.
   - **B** Yes, the child read and took notice of most punctuation.
   - **C** Yes, the child took notice of all punctuation.

Was their pausing appropriate?

5. **Pace** How was the child's pace of reading? Did the pace feel appropriate to the text? We do not recommend that you time the child – remember that pace can be too fast (indicating lack of comprehension) as well as too slow. Instead use your overall impression and judgement as to whether the pace felt right.
   - **A** Either too slow (signalling a lack of automaticity) or too rushed (signalling a lack of comprehension).
   - **B** Fairly good and even, though inappropriately slow or rushed in places.
   - **C** A good, appropriate pace throughout.

Did it sound natural as the child read the text?

Year 2/Primary 3, Summer 2: Fluency Check

Child's name: ______________________ **Date:** __________

Fill in the table below. Use A, B or C to determine specific support that may be required.

A – requires lots of support

B – requires some support

C – requires little to no support

Area of Focus		Consider appropriate support – see page 92.			Comments
		A	B	C	
1	Decoding and Blending				*How many words were overtly sounded and blended after a practice read?*
2	Expression				
3	Smoothness				
4	Punctuation				
5	Pace				

Guidance when deciding on next steps:

Decoding and Blending – ensure that children have adequate rehearsal of code that is secure along with re-reading of texts that have already been accessed. Where children require further support with reading longer words, this can be achieved through repeated rehearsal using the texts from *Fluency Anthology 2* for this half term and the readers listed below.

For this assessment, further practice of these GPCs can be found in Readerful Level 11:

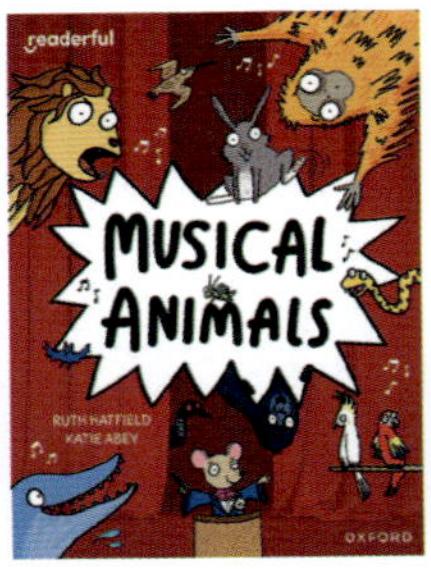

Expression – where appropriate, use 1:1 reading sessions to model and read parts of the text to and with the child. These sessions should take place in addition to group choral or echo reading. All adult reading, whether during lessons or during a protected 'story time' should demonstrate prosody.

Smoothness – additional practice of re-reading texts that use secure code knowledge. Ensure that children re-read texts that contain familiar code. This could mean that they re-read the same texts that were first given to match their current phonic knowledge.

Punctuation and Phrasing – ensure that punctuation and phrasing is explained and its impact on reading is modelled.

Pace – this should be modelled during all teacher-led reading. Re-reading texts will allow children to develop their reading 'at pace' as they become familiar with the text and its content.

There are many factors that can affect a child's reading on any one day. If a child's Fluency Check results don't reflect your knowledge of the child, consider running the check again using the alternative extract or a book at the same level, and use your own judgement when deciding which next steps to follow. The Fluency Check gives you a means of gaining additional information about a child's reading which you can use alongside everything else you know.

If children are not recognising the GPCs that they know in the text, they may require additional support with Blending for Reading. For this, you can use the ELS intervention.

If you recognise that there is a lack of 'fluency' when a child is reading, put in place support that will allow them to develop their reading fluency.

Our roads and public transport have to be properly maintained. This can mean that there are replacement services while the work is taking place.

The company making the repairs must work as quickly as possible. You might see brightly lit signs telling you what is happening. When workers are by the roadside, they must be careful. This means that some road works are done overnight when it is quieter.

The train replacements can sometimes cause disappointment. They can be much slower than the trains! However, if we don't have the tracks replaced or repaired, it could be dangerous.

When the roads and trains are carefully maintained and improvements are made, people often feel relieved. This is because their journeys will hopefully be less stressful. There will be fewer delays. This means their journeys are safer and quicker.

When you see a notice for a road improvement or a train replacement, remember this is to help us. Countless people will have better journeys.

Our public transport services help us to travel with ease. Often, they are better for the environment, too.

Have you ever been on public transport? Have you ever seen a road closed or a train replacement service?

Appendix: List of readers

The following readers were featured in the guidance page following each Progress Check:

Reception Summer 2: Optional Fluency Check

We Can Cook!	Essential Phonic Readers - Level 3	9781382037990
Seeds	Essential Phonic Readers - Level 3	9781382039031
A Shark at the Pool	Essential Phonic Readers - Level 3	9781382038003
A Vet on the Farm	Essential Phonic Readers - Level 3	9781382038010
Rain and Hail	Essential Phonic Readers - Level 3	9781382038027
Night and Light	Essential Phonic Readers - Level 3	9781382038034
Off We Zoom	Essential Phonic Readers - Level 3	9781382039048
A Den in the Woods	Essential Phonic Readers - Level 3	9781382038041
Fix It!	Essential Phonic Readers - Level 3	9781382039055
Joan and the Moon	Essential Phonic Readers - Level 3	9781382038430
Malik and the Owl Cup	Essential Phonic Readers - Level 3	9781382039062
Bats vs Bugs	Essential Phonic Readers - Level 3	9781382039079
The Big Picture	Essential Phonic Readers - Level 3	9781382038454
The Saturn Rocket	Essential Phonic Readers - Level 3	9781382039086
Summer in the Arctic	Essential Phonic Readers - Level 3	9781382038461
On the Reef	Essential Phonic Readers - Level 3	9781382039093
The Pool Frog	Essential Phonic Readers - Level 3	9781382038478
Rabbit in the Well	Essential Phonic Readers - Level 3	9781382039109
Cora the Little Crab	Essential Phonic Readers - Level 3	9781382038485
Is it a Garden?	Essential Phonic Readers - Level 3	9781382039116

Year One/P2 Autumn 1: Fluency Check

The Lost Lunchbox	Essential Phonic Readers - Level 4	9781382038058
Get Fit!	Essential Phonic Readers - Level 4	9781382038065
The Shelter	Essential Phonic Readers - Level 4	9781382038072
In the Summer	Essential Phonic Readers - Level 4	9781382038089
A Good Spot	Essential Phonic Readers - Level 4	9781382038096
Meg's Scrapbook	Essential Phonic Readers - Level 4	9781382039147
All Sorts of Parks	Essential Phonic Readers - Level 4	9781382038102
A Pet Hamster	Essential Phonic Readers - Level 4	9781382039154

Year One/P2 Autumn 2: Fluency Check

The Point Street Garden	Essential Phonic Readers - Level 4	9781382038119
A Fantastic Trip	Essential Phonic Readers - Level 4	9781382039161
A Week at the Coast	Essential Phonic Readers - Level 4	9781382038126
Green Turtles	Essential Phonic Readers - Level 4	9781382039178
Well Played, Saffron!	Essential Phonic Readers - Level 5	9781382038133
Swoop, Creep and Cling	Essential Phonic Readers - Level 5	9781382038140
Beach Clean-Up	Essential Phonic Readers - Level 5	9781382055611
Layla and the Bluebird	Essential Phonic Readers - Level 5	9781382038157
The Snow Birds	Essential Phonic Readers - Level 5	9781382039185
Scout the Lookout	Essential Phonic Readers - Level 5	9781382055628
I Am Like An Elephant	Essential Phonic Readers - Level 5	9781382038164
What's That Smell?	Essential Phonic Readers - Level 5	9781382055635

Year One/P2 Spring 1: Fluency Check

Helping Out	Essential Phonic Readers - Level 5	9781382038171
The Beasts Have a Feast	Essential Phonic Readers - Level 5	9781382055642
A New Home	Essential Phonic Readers - Level 5	9781382038188
Fun Outside	Essential Phonic Readers - Level 5	9781382055659
Putting on a Show	Essential Phonic Readers - Level 5	9781382038195

What Are Feelings?	Essential Phonic Readers - Level 5	9781382039192
Elsy Feels Better	Essential Phonic Readers - Level 5	9781382055666
Feel Good!	Essential Phonic Readers - Level 5	9781382038201
Simran Makes a Splash	Essential Phonic Readers - Level 5	9781382039208
Rock, Cloth or Custard	Essential Phonic Readers - Level 5	9781382055673
The Kite Project	Essential Phonic Readers - Level 5	9781382038218
Is It an Insect?	Essential Phonic Readers - Level 5	9781382039215
The Brightest Star	Essential Phonic Readers - Level 5	9781382055680
Green Pets	Essential Phonic Readers - Level 5	9781382038225
The Lost Den	Essential Phonic Readers - Level 5	9781382039222
Let's Grow a Flower	Essential Phonic Readers - Level 5	9781382055697

Year One/P2 Spring 2: Fluency Check

New Wheels	Essential Phonic Readers - Level 5	9781382038232
Scruffy at the Show	Essential Phonic Readers - Level 5	9781382039239
Lights Out	Essential Phonic Readers - Level 5	9781382055703
The Biggest Pet	Essential Phonic Readers - Level 6	9781382038249
Bring a Thing	Essential Phonic Readers - Level 6	9781382055710
Grow, Tomato, Grow	Essential Phonic Readers - Level 6	9781382038256
The Fun Hunt	Essential Phonic Readers - Level 6	9781382055727
The Night Sky	Essential Phonic Readers - Level 6	9781382038263
Fair Play	Essential Phonic Readers - Level 6	9781382055734
In My Town	Essential Phonic Readers - Level 6	9781382038270
Mighty Matty and Super Seb	Essential Phonic Readers - Level 6	9781382039260
Ask About It	Essential Phonic Readers - Level 6	9781382055741
The Fishing Trip	Essential Phonic Readers - Level 6	9781382038287
Let's Stretch	Essential Phonic Readers - Level 6	9781382055758

Year One/P2 Summer 1: Fluency Check

The Honey Bun Thief	Essential Phonic Readers - Level 6	9781382038294
Tools in Nature	Essential Phonic Readers - Level 6	9781382039277
Escape from the Maze	Essential Phonic Readers - Level 6	9781382055765
All Kinds of Castles	Essential Phonic Readers - Level 6	9781382038300
Record Breaking Birds	Essential Phonic Readers - Level 6	9781382055772
Five Holidays	Essential Phonic Readers - Level 6	9781382038317
Beside the Banyan Tree	Essential Phonic Readers - Level 6	9781382055789
Welcoming Spring	Essential Phonic Readers - Level 6	9781382038324
A Day at the Castle	Essential Phonic Readers - Level 6	9781382055796
The Photo Box	Essential Phonic Readers - Level 6	9781382038331
Where Can Spike Sleep?	Essential Phonic Readers - Level 6	9781382039284
Dec's Super Specs	Essential Phonic Readers - Level 6	9781382055802
All About Instruments	Essential Phonic Readers - Level 6	9781382038348
Beware of the Frog	Essential Phonic Readers - Level 6	9781382055819

Year One/P2 Summer 2: Fluency Check

A World Cookbook	Essential Phonic Readers - Level 6	9781382039291
Jack and the Jellybeans	Essential Phonic Readers - Level 6	9781382055826
The Wrong Cat	Essential Phonic Readers - Level 6	9781382039307
How to Keep Safe Online	Essential Phonic Readers - Level 6	9781382055833
Living Near Volcanoes	Essential Phonic Readers - Level 6	9781382039314
The Ice-Cream Nightmare	Essential Phonic Readers - Level 6	9781382055840
Be A Fossil Hunter	Essential Phonic Readers - Level 6	9781382039321
Ten Top Trains	Essential Phonic Readers - Level 6	9781382055857
Paper Engineer	Essential Phonic Readers - Level 6	9781382039338
Sydney Sneer's Amazing Holiday	Essential Phonic Readers - Level 6	9781382055864

Agnes, The Giant and the Bridge	Essential Phonic Readers - Level 6	9781382039345
Animal Dream Teams	Essential Phonic Readers - Level 6	9781382055871

Year Two/P3 Autumn 1: Fluency Check

Pegasus and Griffin	Essential Phonic Readers - Level 7	9781382039420
How to Make a Video Game	Essential Phonic Readers - Level 7	9781382055888
Big Animals	Essential Phonic Readers - Level 7	9781382039383
Sasha's Sleepover	Essential Phonic Readers - Level 7	9781382055895
The Right Track	Essential Phonic Readers - Level 7	9781382039390
Toxic	Essential Phonic Readers - Level 7	9781382055901
Rock Art	Essential Phonic Readers - Level 7	9781382039406
Beachcombers	Essential Phonic Readers - Level 7	9781382055925
Ant and Grasshopper	Essential Phonic Readers - Level 7	9781382039413
The Missing Map Mystery	Essential Phonic Readers - Level 7	9781382055918
Best Friends	Essential Phonic Readers - Level 7	9781382039376
My City	Essential Phonic Readers - Level 7	9781382055932

Year Two/P3 Autumn 2: Fluency Check

Arthur's Pet Disaster	Essential Phonic Readers - Level 7	9781382055949
Paralympic Power	Essential Phonic Readers - Level 7	9781382055956
Ren and the Special Bowl	Essential Phonic Readers - Level 7	9781382055963
When it Morphs	Essential Phonic Readers - Level 7	9781382055970
Nate's New Room Mate	Essential Phonic Readers - Level 7	9781382055987
Perseverance	Essential Phonic Readers - Level 7	9781382055994

Year Two/P3 Spring 1: Fluency Check

Light in the Dark	Readerful – Level 8	9781382041119
The Art of Colour	Readerful – Level 8	9781382041126
Our Family Farm	Readerful – Level 8	9781382041133
Casper's Art Club	Readerful – Level 8	9781382041140
Bird Tales	Readerful – Level 8	9781382041157
Shackleton – Adventure Awaits	Readerful – Level 8	9781382041164

Year Two/P3 Spring 2: Fluency Check

Feet for Pod	Readerful – Level 9	9781382041232
How old is your Umbrella?	Readerful – Level 9	9781382041249
My Day in A&E	Readerful – Level 9	9781382041256
The Fisher's Mistake	Readerful – Level 9	9781382041263
Mala and the Wish Rocket	Readerful – Level 9	9781382041270
Shackleton - Island Adventure	Readerful – Level 9	9781382041287

Year Two/P3 Summer 1: Fluency Check

Dino Discoveries	Readerful – Level 10	9781382041355
Cave Art Through Time	Readerful – Level 10	9781382041362
Caterpillar Soup and Flying Frogs	Readerful – Level 10	9781382041379
The Ultimate Teacher	Readerful – Level 10	9781382041386
Milly and Mr Minto's Marvellous Music	Readerful – Level 10	9781382041393
Shackleton · Deep Sea Adventure	Readerful – Level 10	9781382041409

Year Two/P3 Summer 2: Fluency Check

Incredible Roads	Readerful – Level 11	9781382041478
Musical Animals	Readerful – Level 11	9781382041485
Amazing Octopuses	Readerful – Level 11	9781382041492
Sonny Works It Out	Readerful – Level 11	9781382041508
Isaac and the Toxics · Robo-Bat Raid	Readerful – Level 11	9781382041515
A Planet Beyond	Readerful – Level 11	9781382041522